The EXTREME Searcher's Guide to
WEB SEARCH ENGINES

The EXTREME Searcher's Guide to
WEB SEARCH ENGINES

A Handbook for the Serious Searcher

2nd Edition

Randolph Hock

Foreword by Reva Basch

CyberAge Books

Information Today, Inc.
Medford, New Jersey

The Extreme Searcher's Guide to Web Search Engines:
A Handbook for the Serious Searcher, Second Edition

Library of Congress Cataloging-in-Publication Data

Hock, Randolph, 1944-
    The extreme searcher's guide to Web search engines : a handbook for the serious searcher / Randolph Hock ; foreword by Reva Basch.-- 2nd ed.
        p. cm.
        ISBN: 0-910965-47-1 (pbk.)
    1. Web search engines.   I. Title
    ZA4226 H63 2001
    025.04--dc21

                                                                                    2001028052

Printed and bound in the United States of America.

Publisher: Thomas H. Hogan, Sr.
Editor-in-Chief: John B. Bryans
Managing Editor: Deborah R. Poulson
Project Editor: John Eichorn
Production Manager: M. Heide Dengler
Cover and book design: Jacqueline Walter and Kara Mia Jalkowski
Indexer: Lori Lathrop

DEDICATION

To Pamela, Matthew, Stephen, and Elizabeth

TABLE OF CONTENTS

LIST OF ILLUSTRATIONS

LiST oF TABLES

FOREWORD

Professional researchers tend to have an attitude about Web search engines. We recognized their limitations immediately: too many hits, not enough precision, and very little control over the process or the output. From the moment we began—some of us reluctantly—to incorporate the Internet into our search toolkits, we gravitated instead toward subject catalogs, meta-sites thick with expertly compiled pointers, and other human-mediated search tools that we hoped would improve our chances of getting relevant, precise, and high-quality results. Search engines, we figured, were for people who didn't know any better. They had their uses, for needle-in-a-haystack questions, for weird or unique terminology, for information we couldn't find any other way. But we resisted—and still do—their claims to index "all" or most of the Web. We dislike the e-commerce come-ons that frame—to the point of obscuring—the simple search-input form we need. And we distrust the "black box" of proprietary search algorithms that determine which documents we do or do not see.

In a way, we're spoiled. Not that life was perfect for those of us who came of age in the pre-Web era of online searching. We had complaints back then as well—about indexing quality; missing, transposed, or flat-out bogus data; and gaps in coverage and content due to licensing constraints, technical problems, or operator error. But we were masters of our search tools. We used proximity operators, internal and end-truncation, set-building, and dozens of system-specific commands. We learned how to recognize data damage and route around it. We used our Boolean wiles to tease from the databases, whatever their flaws, exactly the information we needed.

To say that the commercial databases we searched (and continue to search) were imperfect implies that a standard of perfection exists. The Web has no such standard. Relevance ranking, in all its variant forms, is well-suited to the heterogeneous, sometimes wacky nature of the Net. But its operation is opaque, and opacity does not suit the serious searcher. We're not satisfied with hit-or-miss, mysteriously derived, often-suspect results. We want to know why we got what we got. Casual searchers are happy to take an answer and run, but serious researchers have to satisfy themselves that the answer is valid, or at least representative. They want to know that the results were not biased by some imperfectly understood feature or undocumented limitation of the tools on which they rely.

When I first met Ran Hock, he was a training consultant for one of the leading commercial online services, one highly respected by professionals in business, academia, science, and technology. Like many of us, he had mastered the elements of Boolean logic; knew how to fine-tune proximity operators, field qualifiers, and truncation symbols to guarantee the most relevant results; and could tweak and manipulate little-known system features to guarantee a successful and efficient search.

Hock has brought to this book not only his considerable expertise, but also a set of very high expectations about how a search engine ought to perform. He takes you inside the world of modern search engines, first generally and then systematically, search engine by search engine. Comparative tables and charts, universally applicable search tips, and copious examples make Chapters 1 and 2 a stand-alone resource for smart searching on the Web.

Hock goes on to examine each of the major Web search engines through a serious research lens: What are its strengths and weaknesses? How much of the Web does it cover? How does its default search mode actually operate—in other words, what's inside that black box? How does it stack up in terms of powerful features such as Boolean logic, phrase searching, truncation, and field searching? How does it handle punctuation and uppercase proper names? What are your output options? What extras does it offer—direct access to specialized databases such as maps, stock quotes, or software libraries? A means of refining or narrowing your current search results? Home-page portal features? The ability to customize your view of the site? He also analyzes the structure, content and origin of the subject directories—another way of getting at useful information on the Web—that are part of most search sites today. Each chapter includes annotated screenshots, thumbs-up/thumbs-down ratings, and, at the end, a convenient bite-size summary. Hock covers meta-search engines, both Web- and desktop-based, as well as their peculiar pros and cons. He provides some useful tips for staying current, a glossary, and guidelines for evaluating search engines on your own.

Is the word "extreme" a bit too extreme to apply to the art of searching the Web? Not at all. "Extreme searchers" are similar—perhaps identical—to what I've dubbed "super searchers," a phrase that seems to have made itself at home in the information-professional lexicon. Extreme searchers, like extreme sports enthusiasts, are fearless, focused, committed, and disciplined. In fact, extreme searchers do view research as a sport; they get the same adrenaline rush, the same sense of triumph—or "try-again"—at the end. Pursuing the extreme means knowing how to milk every ounce of performance from your equipment, be it a snowboard, a surfboard, a mountain bike—or a search engine. Ran Hock's book will help you reach, and maintain, the edge.

Reva Basch

Reva Basch is author of Secrets of the Super Searchers, Secrets of the Super Net Searchers, *and* Researching Online For Dummies. *She is also executive editor of the Super Searchers book series.*

ACKNOWLEDGMENTS

As with the first edition of this book, my sincere thanks go to the fine people at Information Today, Inc., for their continued support, encouragement, hard work, and patience. I want to especially thank John Bryans for his continued role in dealing with the "big picture," John Eichorn for his editing expertise and patience, and Janet Spavlik for dealing cheerfully with the challenging formatting and related issues. Thanks are also due to managing editor Deborah Poulson, production manager Heide Dengler, and designers Jacqueline Walter and Kara Mia Jalkowski. I am also particularly grateful to the numerous people on the marketing side who played a big role in making the first edition a success. Not least important, I again thank the boss at Information Today, Inc., Tom Hogan Sr., whom I much admire for the role he has played in the online industry and to whom I continue to be grateful for his support of this book.

I continue to be appreciative of my friends in the New England Online Users Group (NENON) for having suggested the use of the phrase, "Extreme Searcher." Along the same lines, I am grateful to the extreme searchers around the world who are willing and anxious to use search engines to "the extreme" to guarantee the best possible results in fully utilizing the amazing research resources available through the Web.

INTRODUCTION

If you understand adolescents, know one, are one, or have ever been one, it will help you understand where search engines have come since the first edition of this book was published in 1999. They are in late adolescence, growing in size and showing significant signs of maturity, asking themselves, "Who (what) am I?" They're very susceptible to fads, still suffering from growing pains and occasional skin problems. The minor items aside, the biggest change has been growth and maturity. Most search engines had at least doubled or tripled their size by 2001. The maturing process is also obvious. Each search engine has been watching the others and has adopted some of the better behavior (in interfaces and features). Some are indeed asking the identity questions, not quite sure whether they want to be primarily portals or search engines. The susceptibility to some of the minor fads has not completely gone away. (If a minimalist screen with a colorful logo looks good on one engine, another might say, "Let's get one of those.")

Okay, let's not stretch the analogy to the breaking point by getting into the search engine parallels to tattoos, wearing one's cap backwards, and body piercing. The basic analogy, though, still holds. Search engines have been growing and maturing.

In looking at the search engines, this edition will not emphasize what has changed, but what *is*. If you knew them before, you'll recognize the differences anyway. If you're new to the details of these engines, what they used to look like doesn't matter. What the book will aim to do is to help you make the most of what the search engines have to offer, particularly to the "serious searcher."

The concept, aim, and content of this book is hopefully reflected in its title: *The Extreme Searcher's Guide to Web Search Engines: A Handbook for the Serious Searcher.*

The phrase "The Extreme Searcher" addresses the fact that there are many searchers out there who aren't satisfied with the usual, "lowest common denominator" approaches and results. There are many who want and need to stretch the limits of these tools. To be in the category of Extreme Searcher requires no extraordinary skills or training. However, it require (and this book attempts to help provide this) an understanding of the terrain and the equipment.

The term "Web Search Engines" provides some definition of the coverage. For our purposes, a Web search engine is a service provided through the World Wide Web that allows a user to enter a query and search a database that covers a very substantial portion of the Web's content. Being a bit more specific, a search engine allows the user to enter one or more terms, with optional qualifiers, in order to locate Web pages of interest. The term is almost interchangeable with "Web search services," which in this book will usually refer more to the overall site, and which in turn may provide the search engine as one of multiple options. The search engine may even be just one offering in a collection of offerings that together aim to provide the user with a general starting place or "portal" to the Web.

The "guide" and "handbook" aspects of this book further define the intent. This book attempts to organize and make easily accessible that material which is necessary for effective searching. It does not intend to include all the minutiae and the theoretical issues relating to Web search engines, but rather focus on the practical—on knowledge that's useful and necessary for finding relevant answers quickly.

The "serious searcher" referred to is a variation on the "extreme searcher" theme, but with emphasis on purpose. The phrase is meant to help define the probable audience, and refers to those search engine users who make frequent use of the Web for business, scientific, technical, and other research purposes. These are the people (you, hopefully) who need greater retrieval capabilities than those that can be realized by using the simplest versions and approaches provided by the search engine services. Most of these services, though, focus primarily on what Infoseek once described as "the average, nontechnical consumer." Though such users can make very effective use of the simplest approaches to searching, there is indeed tremendous retrieval power that can be utilized with just a little increase in effort and knowledge.

More specifically, this book aims to facilitate more effective and efficient use of Web search engines by helping the reader:

- Know the basic structure of the major search engines
- Become acquainted with those attributes (features, benefits, options, content, etc.) that search engines have in common and where they differ

- Know the main strengths and weaknesses of the major search engines
- Pick up some tips, tricks, and techniques that can contribute to more effective and easier searching

These aims are addressed in a general manner in Chapter One, "Search Engines in General," and Chapter Two, "Common Searching Options." Chapter One takes a very brief look at the history of Web search engines and goes into a bit more detail on how they're put together. Chapter Two addresses search features and options that are found across and among the engines.

Chapters Three through Ten include profiles of eight leading search engines. These eight were chosen based on their size and their prominence and/or strength as research tools. Yahoo!, though structured primarily as a directory rather than a search engine, is also included because, with its integration of results from the large Google database, it also can legitimately be categorized as a search engine. In these chapters, much more emphasis is given to the service's "searching" features than to the numerous and quite varied portal features that often are not very closely related to the main "searching" function of the engine. The Web "directories" that are attached to many of the search engines are given a little more attention than other portal features, largely because of the increased degree to which directory content is automatically incorporated into search results. Each profile is designed to allow the searcher to easily grasp what the engine has to offer and how to take advantage of that.

In the first edition of this book, WebCrawler was included, mainly out of respect for its history as the first widely used Web search engine. Since its content is now minuscule and it now provides little utility for the serious searcher, it has been dropped from this edition. Go.com was likewise dropped. When its substantial redesign was introduced in mid-2000, its producers announced that the new Go.com would focus primarily on entertainment and leisure, putting it outside the intended scope of this book. The redesign also eliminated four of the seven items that were to be listed as its "Strengths." In addition, the size of its database at that point was substantially less than 100 million records, no longer in the same league as the rest of the search engines covered.

Chapters have been added for two important recent additions to the search engine field, Google and Fast Search. Their size, uniqueness, and retrieval power place them in the "must-know" category. Two other new search engines were seriously considered for addition, MSN Search and NBCi.com (formerly SNAP). Neither of these, however, provides any particularly unique or strong contribution to the serious searcher's arsenal and it was decided not to cover them here.

Chapter Twelve provides an overview and sampling of the numerous meta-search engines, exploring what they have to offer, but also providing some cautions as to what they do not offer.

Chapter Thirteen talks about the other Web search engines that are out there and where to find out about them. It also addresses the issue of "keeping up" and provides some suggested sources for doing so.

On the subject of keeping up, the author is providing a Web page to address the changes that will inevitably take place as they relate to the content of this book. (See "About the Extreme Searcher's Web Page" that follows this introduction.)

Since the first edition of this book, search engines have ironed out some of their wrinkles and eliminated some of their flaws. That doesn't mean, however, that you won't still find some problem areas. If things don't behave as you expect, it's probably not because you are doing anything wrong. Possibly it's because the engines sometimes don't deliver on their producers' claims and they don't always do things the way an experienced, serious searcher would like them to—or for that matter, what their documentation says. Facing these facts can make a happier, healthier searcher. The vast majority of the claims and features do, though, work as claimed, and can provide quick and easy access to hundreds of millions of useful Web pages in the WWW universe.

One final introductory comment at the "universal" level: The comparison of the Digital Revolution to the Industrial Revolution is not an exaggeration. The wealth of resources that the Web provides to the world is nothing short of amazing, and Web search engines are arguably the most effective tool the serious searcher has for accessing this wealth. Enjoy and profit from being an active participant in this exciting time.

ABOUT THE EXTREME SEARCHER'S WEB PAGE
www.extremesearcher.com

The World Wide Web and the search engines that provide access to it are constantly changing. For search engines there are both cosmetic changes and substantive changes and, in the latter category, it's most frequently an added feature, rather than a change in how you do things with the existing features. For that reason, most of what's included in this book should remain valid for a fairly long period. To keep up on changes, however, readers are provided with The Extreme Searcher's Web Page. This resource provides information on what's new and what has changed. The emphasis is on those changes that affect how you can get the most effective retrieval from these engines. The site also provides a collection of links to the engines and to the online resources mentioned in Chapter Twelve.

The Extreme Searcher's Web Page is available to you as a valued reader of *The Extreme Searcher's Guide to Web Search Engines.* To access it, go to www.extremesearcher.com.

Enjoy your visit there and please send any feedback by e-mail to ran@extremesearcher.com.

CHAPTER 1

Search Engines in General

A VERY BRIEF HISTORY

Web search engines have a very brief history, less than a decade, and this brief section is a very brief summary of that brief history.

Before there were Web search engines, there was chaos. If you wanted to find something on the Internet you needed to know its exact address. The first really significant step out of that chaos and toward a degree of organization of Internet content was the development of "gophers," server-based collections of Internet addresses arranged in a menu format. (The term "gopher" comes from the mascot for the University of Minnesota, from whence the first Internet "gopher" emerged.) Gophers were non-HTML-based and typically indexed not much more than file titles or very brief descriptions, but if you knew how to get to a gopher it would allow you to download selected files. Gophers begat Archie (which searched gophers) and Archie begat Veronica (which searched all of "gopherspace") and Veronica begat Jughead, but by that time they had become less relevant than even the comic strip characters after which they were named and few people even got around to figuring out what Jughead was.

The gopher lineage was barely more than a couple of years old when it was overshadowed by the rapid development of the World Wide Web, which allowed exploitation of hyperlinks, full-text searching,

1

graphical browsers, and other easy-to-use and highly interactive technology—and the development of Web search engines.

The first successful Web search engine to emerge was WebCrawler, which came from the University of Washington and made its public debut in April 1994. Within a year three competitors were on the scene: Lycos, Infoseek, and OpenText. In late 1995 AltaVista and Excite appeared. Interestingly, much, maybe most, of the actual searching technology of use to the serious searcher today was already present in varying degrees in these earlier search engines, including features such as Boolean, truncation, etc. Unfortunately—and the impact of this continues into the present—none of these search engines took advantage of the heavy-duty searching technology and approaches found in online services such as DIALOG and LEXIS-NEXIS. Additionally, neither the search engines nor their cousins, the Web directories, took advantage of the extensive subject classification theory and practice of the last hundred or so years. These points are relevant in a very practical way in that the serious searcher must recognize that most Web search engines were and are developed for the more casual searcher, not for those who are anxious to take advantage of more sophisticated approaches and techniques.

HotBot came along in 1996 and Northern Light in 1997. HotBot brought a more sophisticated yet easy-to-use interface coupled with a very large database (by the end of 1997, it was the largest available). Northern Light brought an integration of Web searching and searching of proprietary information. Google appeared in 1998, and its "popularity-based" ranking of records and an ultra-simple interface were effectively combined to produce an engine that quickly achieved popularity among both casual and longtime searchers. Meanwhile, the race to be the largest search engine had abated somewhat until the appearance in 1999 of Fast Search, which claimed a database of over 200 million records. This impetus, along with other competitive factors, meant the race for size was on again, with four engines having hit the 200-million-record mark by January 2000.

Among the "early" search engines, Open Text was the first to bite the dust. By early 1998 it was no longer available. There will probably be more disappearances over the next two or three years, and probably the appearance of at least one or two more major search engines. In the meantime, the changes within current engines continue, though many of these are largely either fairly superficial or more a part of the "portal" nature of the service than an integral part of the "searching" aspect. (More on the portal aspect later.) We can hope that the producers of these tools will continue working on enhancing search capabilities, and there are indications that the competitive aspects will continue to nudge this along. In a few cases, it will be a step in the right direction if the engine just begins to fulfill its promises.

As with the rest of the business world, search engine companies are extremely susceptible to fads. In 1996 and 1997, the fad was to make sure that your engine had an "advanced" version, regardless of whether the advanced version really did anything more sophisticated or whether the same things could not have been incorporated into the main home page.

Of more significance in terms of benefits, 1998 brought "personalization" and "portalization." The personalized portal or "Web gateway" idea manifested itself in localized and user-selected news categories appearing on the home page, local weather and TV listings, personal stock portfolio tracking, personal calendars, etc. (Yes, horoscopes, too.) Nourished by the search engine producers' desire to follow the lead of others and the realization that this approach was something that could attract advertising revenues, these two closely related models quickly became the almost-universal business model for the major search engines. Though many users had not yet realized it, this portalization/personalization approach was a major step forward in terms of really bringing the Web to the level of a household and desktop "appliance"—one that's always at hand, uncomplicated, used frequently, and, most importantly, providing concrete and obvious benefits.

The years 1999 and 2000 brought a more subtle and less heralded, but very powerful, corollary to the portal concept. In the first year or so of portals, the added tools (such as directories, etc.) were mainly just laid out on the home page with the hope that people would use them. In 1999 there was a major shift toward automatically incorporating the content of these "add-ons" into the results pages—at the same time the search engine's Web database is searched, it searches the subject directory, the company directory, etc., and presents those results along with the regular search results. This integration of resources has significantly improved the quality of search results by seamlessly providing the searcher with output that's highly relevant and that comes without having to perform the search separately in several tools. For the low price of nothing you can get a search not just of the Web index, but a Web directory search, a company directory search, a dictionary search, etc.—a little bit like the "cross-file" searching in some of the older, commercial online database services.

The next step is up to the users as much as to the search engine producers. The tools that receive user attention will be retained, enhanced, copied, and valued. The problem, as from the beginning with Web search engines, is that the person likely to be reading this book (the extreme searcher), and who needs the features and tools emphasized by this book, is not the typical search engine user. The "typical" user could care less about the more sophisticated and research-oriented features. The degree to which this is true is very evident if you look at typical searches. Lycos provides an interesting, though sometimes depressing, list of favorite searches. In a typical week, the top 50 searches include 46 that are in the entertainment, sports, or games categories. The relevance of this is not an issue of elitism, or information snobbery, but the need to face the reality that the main place most search engines make money is not with the researcher using the Web for professional purposes. The good news is that the overall audience is increasing, and the number of people who use search engines for professional purposes, for investing, and for increased literacy on such topics as science, humanities, business, and medicine, is perhaps increasing more rapidly. The number of searches for

"Worldwide Wrestling Federation" isn't likely to decrease. However, the number of, shall we say, "more intellectually valuable" searches is increasing. There are more reasons for the search engine producers to pay attention to the extreme searcher. But the serious searcher also needs to use an engine's more serious features so that those features will stay around and be enhanced.

HOW SEARCH ENGINES ARE PUT TOGETHER

Since discussions of search engines naturally lead dangerously close to an automotive metaphor, we might as well give in and go with that metaphor briefly. A danger is that some readers already may be saying to themselves, "I don't care what's under the hood of my vehicle, I just want to know how to drive it." Quite honestly, this book is not intended for the "driver" who doesn't care to know how to check the oil. It's intended for the researcher who wants to know at least a little more than the basics, who cares about taking a few extra steps that may very significantly improve the performance of his or her searching. To do that, it's necessary to understand some things about how search engines are put together.

Before we can talk about the structure of search engines, it's important to address the context in which they are now more often than not placed: the portal. The idea behind portals is that there can be a primary page (site) on the Web that a user automatically goes to first and that provides an easy gateway to that user's most-needed tools. This gateway (portal) lays out a collection of frequently needed information and tools that save the user from having to look in several different places. For example, by using a personalized Excite page as my browser's "start page," in one place I can see selected categories of news headlines, my local weather forecast, my stock portfolio, my calendar of upcoming engagements, etc. Most importantly, in the context of this book, I see the query box for the site's search engine, the box that allows me to query the database of over 200 million Web sites. We'll be looking primarily at that part of these sites, the search engine itself, but not ignoring the other portal features, especially when they contribute significantly to better results for a search query.

Unfortunately, in common usage the term "search engine" has, because of its origins, come to refer to both the service's entire site and the part of that site that accepts queries and searches the large Web database. In most cases, the term "search engine" here will be referring to the latter, and "service" or "portal" will refer to the entire site. "Portal features" will be used to refer to the other tools and information provided (directories, weather, etc.). Maybe we'd better run through that one time: The AltaVista *service* provides a *portal* that includes a *search engine* and other portal features such as news, a Web directory, and other tools.

The search engine itself can be considered to have five main functional parts: (1) the engine's "crawlers," which go out and find Web sites and pages; (2) the database of information gathered about those pages and about other pages that have been gathered from other sources; (3) the indexing program, which indexes the content of the database; (4) the "retrieval engine," the algorithm and associated programming, devices, etc. that, upon request, retrieve material from the index/database; and (5) the graphical (HTML) interface, which gathers query data from the user to feed to the retrieval engine.

Because of the increased degree to which portal features are being integrated into the searching process, it actually would be legitimate to consider some portal features as a sixth main part.

Crawlers

Crawlers, or *spiders*, are the programs that go out to the Web to (1) identify new sites that are to be added to the search engine and (2) to identify sites already covered that have changed. Crawlers gather information about the content of pages from sites and feed that information to the search engine's database. Much could be said about how this happens, but for the searcher just a few points are relevant and provide an understanding of why some engines find certain pages and other engines miss those pages, even when the page is in the second engine's database. For many engines, more popular sites (such as those that are clicked on frequently by users and those that have lots of links *to* them) are probably crawled more thoroughly and more frequently than less-popular sites. Crawlers can be programmed for *depth* or for *breadth*, or both. Those programmed for depth not only identify main sites, but identify the subsidiary pages to the main page, the subsidiary pages of those pages, etc. Crawlers programmed for *breadth* of sites are typically concerned with finding more main sites, but not necessarily identifying all the subsidiary pages of a site. As search engines have matured and become even more competitive, there has been a tendency to see a greater melding of both depth and breadth.

The Engine's Database

The total collection of information that's stored about all the individual Web pages constitutes the search engine's database. The collection includes pages that have been identified by crawlers but increasingly also includes pages identified by other sources or techniques. A very large number of sites added to search engines come from direct submissions by Web page publishers. If you examine any search engine's home page, you will probably find a link that allows you or anyone else to submit a page to the search engine. As long as the page is not just a case of "spamming," pages submitted will probably be added to the database. All or most search engine producers examine submitted pages for spam (nasty little tricks used by nasty little programmers to illegitimately increase a page's chances of being retrieved). A service may also apply other criteria but, with the exception of spam, chances are very good that a submitted page will end up in the engine's database.

Other sources may also feed into the search engine's database. The database may, for example, include pages and/or subject headings from a directory such as Open Directory or Yahoo!.

(Note: In this discussion we're using the words "site" and "page" somewhat interchangeably. Technically speaking, a "site," usually thought of as corresponding to a particular domain name, can have many pages—even thousands of them.)

It's sometimes easy to forget that when we're using a search engine, we're not directly searching the Web, but rather searching a database that contains records describing a portion of those pages that exist on the Web. Remembering this can help avoid unrealistic expectations about what a search engine can actually accomplish.

The Indexing Program and the Index

In terms of which pages will actually be retrieved by a query, indexing can be even more critical than the crawling process. The indexing program examines the information stored in the database and creates the appropriate entries in the index. When you submit a query, it is this index that's used in order to identify matching records.

Most search engines claim to index "all" of the words from every page. The catch is what the engines choose to regard as a "word." Some have a list of "stop words" (small, common words that are considered insignificant enough to be ignored) that they don't index. Some leave out such obvious candidates as articles and conjunctions. Some leave out other high-frequency but potentially valuable words such as "Web" and "Internet." Sometimes numerals are left out, making it difficult, for example, to search for "Troop 13." The good news is that over the last couple years, in general, search engines have been treating fewer words as stop words and the "Troop 13" search will work in more engines than previously.

All major engines index the "high value" fields such as the title and the URL. Metatags are usually indexed, but not always. (Metatags are words, phrases, or sentences that are placed in a special section of the HTML (Hypertext Markup Language) code as a way of describing the content of the page. Metatags are not displayed when you view a page, though you can view them if you wish by telling your browser to show the "page source." For those who don't know HTML, viewing the page source for a page or two can be an informative and worthwhile exercise.) Without much imagination, it's easy to see how useful the content of metatags is for information retrieval. However, some engines purposely do *not* index some metatags because metatags are the part of the page that's most susceptible to abuse by spammers. This caution is taken at the considerable expense of ignoring extremely valuable indexing information.

Those familiar with HTML know that frames are used in millions of sites. (Frames are an HTML device that treats different parts of a page as somewhat independent "windows" or window "panes.") Some search engines do not index frames, thereby causing the searcher the possible loss of some relevant sites. This weakness is somewhat compensated for by the fact that the astute Web page developer will create a "no frames" version of the site as well as the frames version. In addition, with the evolution of Web page building, frames are being used less frequently than they were in the past.

Some search engines index the words in hypertext anchors and links (e.g., "Click Here"), names of Java "applets," links within image maps, etc. Other search engines do not. Understanding that there are these variations in indexing policy goes a long way toward explaining why relevant pages, even when in the search engine's database, may not be retrieved by some searches. It also explains why a page may be retrieved by one engine and not another, even when the same page is in both engines.

The Retrieval Engine

This is the program that receives your query and then searches the index to identify and deliver the records that match your query. In effect, two major things happen as part of this process: (1) the retrieval engine identifies the matching records by means of a "retrieval algorithm," and (2) the engine then arranges the retrieved items in a particular order to be displayed to the user. These may happen more or less simultaneously, or they may be fairly distinct operations.

Retrieval algorithms are discussed in some detail later on. For the moment, we will just say that these programs utilize matching criteria to determine which records contain particular words, phrases, or combinations thereof. They may also match other user-specified criteria, such as whether a particular page contains audio or image files.

The part of the search engine that estimates relevance of records may be closely integrated into the retrieval algorithm or it may be a separate process. Even when it's a fairly separate process, the separateness may not be obvious to the user, and usually doesn't need to be. In some cases, the fact that two processes are occurring may be obvious, such as with AltaVista's Advanced Search, where the user must specify, in the separate "Sort by" box, that relevance ranking should occur.

The HTML Interface

What users see when they connect with a search engine is the HTML-based *interface*. This interface gathers query data from the user, and sends that data to the search engine for it to do the retrieval. Its most obvious function is to provide a means for the user to specify the query. However, the interface also serves several other functions, including providing a space for advertisers (which consequently generates revenue for the search engine company), providing access to the various portal features, and providing links to "Help" pages and other information about the service.

THE DATABASES BEHIND THE DATABASES

Having described the preceding parts of a typical search engine, it's now necessary to complicate the picture a bit and point out that not all search engines create their own databases. Some search engines rely on databases created by third parties, then add their additional special content, features, ranking algorithms, interfaces, etc. Most prominently, several search engines (such as HotBot and MSN Search) make use of Inktomi. Inktomi (with 500 million records) has done the crawling and indexing, and access to the resultant database is sold to HotBot and others. Those search engines then can manipulate the database, provide varying points of access (field searching), and, if they wish, meld the results of the Inktomi database search with results from other sources. Consequently, searching two search engines, both of which may use Inktomi, may produce different results.

Fast Search also provides its database to others, and for the time being (unlike Inktomi) also enables access directly through its own site. The first major search engine to make use of the Fast Search database is Lycos, but expect others to follow.

PORTAL FEATURES

In the first edition of this book, this section was labeled "Add-Ons"—and therein lies an important point. The features we're referring to are those additional tools and information items appearing on the service's interface that are not necessarily a part of the Web "searching" function—Web directories, news, company directories, stock information, maps, weather, etc. (For our present purposes, we're defining the "searching" function as the process where a user enters specific criteria and the service searches a database to identify and return Web pages that match the criteria.)

When the portal concept first began to be developed by Web search services, most of the non-searching features were pretty much just "added-on." They weren't very closely integrated with the searching function and many of the benefits they provided could be obtained in better form elsewhere.

Perhaps the first good example of effective *integration* of Web database searching with one of these other tools is Yahoo!, where the searching function and the directory functions were integrated early on. Yahoo! is more often thought of as a directory (a browsable, categorized, and selective collection) than as a general Web search engine, but because of the degree of integration of the two functions it has always deserved a seat in both camps. Yahoo! integrates browsing particularly well because, when "searching" in Yahoo!, Yahoo!'s classification headings are searched and when "browsing" at any of the levels within the classification scheme, the searcher can choose to "search" just within that category. Yahoo! further integrated resources by providing the option of automatically searching not just its own database but also a larger Web database (first AltaVista and now Google). With the "portalization" of Web search services, the majority of services have moved toward this kind of integration of tools. As we will see, the integration applies not just to the integration of search and Web directory resources, but to other tools as well.

A final major point to consider when examining the benefits of a portal is the ability of the user to personalize the home page. Most Web search services that provide portal features also allow you to customize your page. (The same is true for other kinds of portals than Web search portals. News sites, such as MSNBC and CNN, also provide more than just their own news and make their sites personalizable.) If you haven't personalized at least one search engine home page, put down this book and do it now! By doing so, when you log on you will see your own selection of categories of news headlines, your local weather, and your own stock portfolio. With only a little more effort, you can personalize such things as your own list of upcoming meetings, sports scores only for the teams you follow, and your local TV listings.

In the chapters on the individual services, the portal features will be identified and discussed to varying degrees, depending on how integrated they are with the searching, or how unique, useful, and interesting the feature is. Attempts are made in both Table 1.1 and the index at the end of this book to provide ways for you to easily identify which engines have a particular portal feature or type of feature.

Table 1.1 lists the more common portal features and identifies which are available within the Web search services. A check mark indicates that the feature is available either on the site's regular home page or on the personalized home page. Be aware that these change constantly, so periodically take a close look at search service home pages to see if some new useful features have appeared.

Table 1.1 Inclusion of typical portal features by the major search engines							
	Alta-Vista	Excite	Fast Search	Google	HotBot	Lycos	Northern Light	Yahoo!
Personalizable Page		✓			✓-	✓		✓
Web Directory	✓	✓		✓	✓	✓	✓	✓
Yellow Pages	✓	✓			✓	✓		✓
White Pages	✓	✓			✓	✓		✓
Image Search	✓	✓	✓		✓	✓		
Audio/Video Search	✓	✓	✓		✓	✓		
News	✓	✓			✓	✓	✓	✓
Weather		✓				✓		✓
Sports		✓				✓		✓
Stocks		✓			✓	✓	✓	✓
Maps/Directions	✓	✓			✓	✓		✓
Shopping	✓	✓			✓	✓		✓
Horoscope		✓				✓		✓
TV Listings		✓				✓		✓

Table 1.1 Inclusion of typical portal features by the major search engines (*cont.*)

	Alta-Vista	Excite	Fast Search	Google	HotBot	Lycos	Northern Light	Yahoo!
Calendar		✓			✓	✓		✓
Address Book		✓						✓
Family Filter	✓		✓	✓		✓		✓
International Versions	✓	✓		✓		✓		✓
Translation	✓					✓		
Alerts		✓					✓	✓
COMMUNICATION SERVICES								
Free Home Pages						✓		✓
Free ISP		✓				✓		
Free E-mail	✓	✓				✓		✓
Free Voice Mail		✓				✓		✓
Discussion Groups/ Message Boards		✓			✓	✓		✓
Chat		✓				✓		✓

The fact that the portal aspect of these services is treated secondarily to the search function is not to say that the former is less important than the latter. Portals are treated that way because the aim of this book is to address effective Web *searching*, and what is said about portals will be in that context of searching rather than vice versa. Indeed, every searcher should consider and take advantage of what the portal concept offers. We don't just go on the Web to search. For many people, the selection, customization, and use of a portal is what, one day soon, will make accessing the Web a more frequent occurrence than picking up the telephone.

COMPONENTS OF A TYPICAL SEARCH ENGINE HOME PAGE

Whether a Web search service is primarily portal- or search-oriented, the visual appearance of the home pages differs tremendously. This is actually somewhat beneficial to the searcher as a way of obtaining a mental image of each of the various services. However, until one has gotten fairly intimate with several of the engines, the lack of consistency can add confusion. For this reason, it will be worthwhile to look at a "typical" search engine service home page to identify the content and features that the services tend to have in common. Once the similarities are seen, it's easy to take a quick look at any search engine service and get a feel for what can be done with it.

AltaVista contains most of the elements typically found on search engine home pages. See Figure 1.1.

Database Options

Some search engines provide a choice of what collection of sources is to be searched. The options may include a search of the service's main Web database or searches of other collections (databases), such as images, audio and video, proprietary journal literature, and discussion groups.

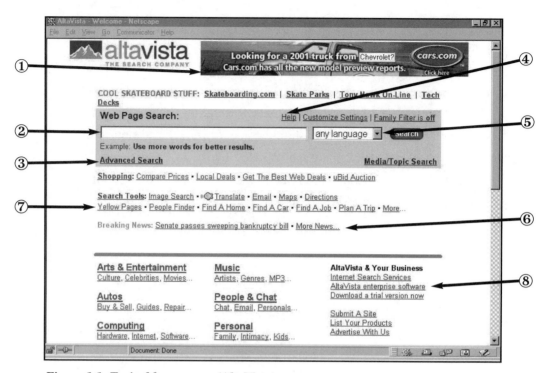

Figure 1.1 Typical home page (AltaVista)

① Advertisement ⑤ Search Options
② Query box ⑥ News
③ Link to Advanced Search ⑦ Other Portal Features
④ Help Links ⑧ Site Promotion

The default and most obvious choice is "the Web," meaning all of the Web pages included within the database of that search service. Often a text box or radio buttons are provided for search options. When this is the case, alternatives offered are usually ones for which search features and structure are similar to that for the Web search.

Frequently, there will be links elsewhere on the page for searching other databases (such as stock information databases), but for these links the search engine used is usually different and often provided by another company. For example, Excite provides such a link for stock quotes and weather, each of which lead to very different looking interface pages.

Query Box(es)

These boxes are the heart of it all since it is here where you enter your query. Exactly what you can enter (phrases, Boolean logic, etc.) depends upon the search engine. (Boolean logic, discussed in the next chapter, is in this context the capability of using "operators" such as +, -, AND, OR, and NOT to retrieve only those records that have a particular combination of terms.)

Query Modifier Options

About half of the search engines provide some option on the home page for modifying your query. The options are most often presented either as a pull-down window, radio buttons, or check boxes. They provide options for qualifying the search by language, date, special content, applying Boolean operators, etc.

Link to the Advanced Version

For all engines that provide an advanced-version option, there will be a link somewhere on the home page that leads to the more advanced version. Often the link itself is surprisingly small, almost as if they really don't want you to see it. Keep in mind that if you prefer the advanced version, you can just bookmark the advanced version's page rather than, or in addition to, the service's main home page.

Advertising

Advertising on search engines is almost inevitable. For most companies that provide these search engines, advertising and licensing of their software provide the main revenue stream from search engine operations. (If you hadn't noticed it, the fact that the ads are related to your search topic isn't just an amazing coincidence. If you do a search that includes the word "furniture," an ad for a furniture store pops up. The advertiser has paid for that to happen. If you look at it from a positive perspective, this very targeted advertising can be beneficial to the consumer as well as the advertiser. I wish the junk mail that comes through the postal service were as relevant.)

Directory (Topics, Channels, Classification)

For the major engines, extensive listings of additional Web information resources usually appear in one of the following formats (or as a variation on one of the following):

- "Directory," or a classified list of selected sites. Keep in mind that in each engine, these "selected" sites constitute only a small portion of the number of sites found in the Web database of the search engine. Some of the search engines have a directory they have created and maintain themselves, while others use a directory that's made available to several engines. Currently, Open Directory (available in its "native" form at www.dmoz.org) and LookSmart (LookSmart.com) are the directories of choice for several search engines.

  Since Open Directory is the more research-oriented directory encountered, it's worthwhile to go into a little detail about it here, rather than repeat that detail in each of the search engines that use it. Open Directory is the largest of the Web directories, with over 2 million records. Unlike Yahoo!, with several hundred paid editors, Open Directory uses volunteer editors—over 30,000 of them. On the one hand, this could mean more variable quality in their choices of sites, but on the other it means that many of the editors are much more experienced in their specific areas than Yahoo! editors can be. On the whole, the quality of the content seems to be quite good and a good page is more likely to quickly get into Open Directory than into Yahoo!. Open Directory has 15 top-level categories, and most categories/subcategories go down four or five levels. It contains cross-references and descriptions ("scope notes") for categories, and allows searching within each level of the hierarchy as well as at the top level. Individual search engines implement Open Directory somewhat differently

- "Channels," or specialized pages on particular broad topics such as business, entertainment, or sports. Each of these pages may contain directory listings for that topic, searchable sites, etc. In Excite, for example, under the Business category, you'll find a link to the Business section of Excite's directory, a stock quote search, company directories, a collection of online business tools, and a variety of other business-related links.

Site Promotion

This is where the search engine producer puts in its plug for how great the search service is. It usually highlights special features or content, so at least glance at this occasionally. The services use this area to point out some interesting features that might otherwise be missed.

Other Portal Features

This category covers the numerous and varied features such as those listed in Table 1.1.

Help Links

This will lead you to one or more pages that tell how the search engine allegedly works. While most of what you read in the help pages will be correct, unfortunately, some services occasionally promise things they don't really deliver. In some cases the services provide features that aren't documented in the help screens. Some services have been known to make major changes without taking the time to update their help screens. In general, the help screens are done conscientiously and the quality has continued to improve.

> **Tip: Learn two or three engines well, but use the others frequently.**

What to Realistically Expect from These Services

Especially for those who have extensively searched such online services as DIALOG and LEXIS-NEXIS, expectations for Web search engines may need to be tempered considerably. The variety of features, the sophistication and reliability of features, and, in some cases, the reliability of retrieval provided by Web search engines still are often not up to par with that provided by those established commercial services. The very nature of general Web search engines, particularly their goal of reaching tens of millions of users, at the moment precludes the level of customer support one expects from those older services.

However, the level of tolerance of such shortcomings can be significantly raised when we remind ourselves that the Web search services are FREE! There are no per-minute charges, no subscription charges, and no output charges.

The gap between traditional retrieval expectations and Web search expectations is further narrowed when a couple of other factors are considered. Recognition of both of these factors is important for the searcher who wants to get the most out of either kind of search service.

First, Web search engines are dealing with very unstructured data, or at least data with very little consistency of structure. Indeed, there is a definite structure to the HTML behind the Web pages, but for the actual intellectual content, about the only "intellectual" structure is found in the titles and metatags. The body of the pages has little consistent structure that the Web search service can use for structured searching. This situation will change as Web page builders begin to make better use of options such as XML (eXtensible Markup Language), which provides virtually unlimited identification of the various kinds of data that might exist on a page. Some search engines are prepared to take advantage of this and are just waiting for sites to provide them with this kind of structure within pages.

Second, the sheer volume of data currently on the Web—in combination with the volume added every day—should add a degree of respect for what the Web search engines have accomplished in a very short period of time. The fact that there's at least an elementary level of access to the hundreds of millions of pages of material is a feat that should inspire much more awe than disappointment.

In a July 1999 article ("Accessibility of Information on the Web," *Nature* 400:107-109, 1999), Steve Lawrence and C. L. Giles reported on their continuing study of the degree to which search engines cover the total content of the Web. In the article, the researchers estimated that the Web at that point contained 800 million pages of information and that the major search engines each covered well less than a quarter of that material. They estimated that of the 800 million pages, Northern Light covers only 16 percent, SNAP and AltaVista 15.5 percent, HotBot 11 percent, and for the others they studied, less than 10 percent each.

It should be pointed out that their numbers are not accepted by all observers. Some search engine producers, in particular, feel that the numbers given are greatly inflated by the fact that a very large number of the pages counted in the study are actually duplicates, with different URLs really referring to the same page (e.g., www.onstrat.com and onstrat.com), or actual duplicates of the same page on different servers, etc. Plus, a large portion is spam. If these observers are correct, Web search engines actually are covering a much larger proportion of the Web than indicated by the Lawrence and Giles study.

Whichever is correct, to add some perspective to those numbers, keep in mind that covering even a fourth or so of the published Web pages may actually be pretty good. Though there are of course the big issues of selectivity and quality to consider, in regard to extent of coverage consider that the more traditional indexing services have never covered anywhere near those percentages of "published" material. Respected services such as *Chemical Abstracts, Psychological Abstracts,* and others don't even make an attempt to cover everything published that makes mention of, respectively, chemistry or psychology. In a nutshell, take advantage of what the Web search engines do cover, and search more than one engine when you want to retrieve as much on your topic as possible.

Even when several engines are searched, be aware that there is one very large portion of the Web that search engines at present cannot cover: the so-called "invisible Web." These are primarily Web pages that lie behind password-protected sites and/or pages that are part of databases that require user input in order to be searched. To access the content of these databases, you must either register and enter a password and/or enter a query on a search page found at the site. If you need access to the pages contained in these sites, you need to go directly to the site, rather than attempt to search them using a general Web search engine. For an excellent collection of links to this type of site, take a look at the Direct Search site compiled by Gary Price of George Washington University (gwis2.circ. gwu.edu/~gprice/direct.htm).

For a reasonable set of expectations regarding *searchability*, there is one overreaching aspect that needs to be considered. In general, most Web search engines are not designed for the *serious* searcher. For the most part, they are designed for the casual user, not the person who needs to apply what they retrieve in the business and research environment. When a search engine's documentation uses *Baywatch* stars in its search examples, we get a sense of their assumed audience. Facing this fact while at the same time making the best use of what *is* offered can prove to be the prudent approach. If serious users take advantage of the more sophisticated features offered, more sophisticated features may follow. With the number of competing search engines catering to the casual searcher, some may break away and target those who need heavier-duty retrieval power. Indeed, we've already seen this happen in the case of Northern Light. Other search engines have also begun to at least take greater note of the needs of the "extreme searcher."

There are some other things *not* to expect:

- Consistency from one search engine to another. This can be seen as more of a positive than a negative as it's too early in the game to come to definitive conclusions about what are the best ways to provide Web searching.

- The traditional tools you're used to with the older online vendors (such as controlled vocabulary, full range of Boolean and proximity connectors, tailored output formats, etc.)

- Comprehensive bibliographic searching—For listings of what has been published in journals, books, technical reports, dissertations, etc., the Web search engines will still not provide even moderately definitive results, especially for retrospective searches. For many subject areas, the best bet for bibliographic searching is to either use one of the commercial services or find a database on the Web, such as ERIC (the database for the education literature), that covers your area of interest.

- To know what's happening during the search. Experienced online researchers often like to know all the finer details of what's happening behind the scenes so that they can get a good sense of whether they're really accomplishing their retrieval goals. Exactly what's happening behind the scenes is considered very proprietary by the Web search services (for competitive purposes) and this, in combination with some obvious inconsistencies, means that extensive knowledge of the details is usually not achievable. (In terms of my own desire to know every last little detail of what is happening, my own advice to myself is, "Get over it.")

Finally, *don't* expect all the specifics you learn about any particular search engine today to be true tomorrow. Rather, learn what factors are involved in the searching process so you can interpret what you are seeing and so you can make the next move in a reasoned manner.

Subjects/Areas Covered by Search Engines

For none of the search engines profiled in detail here is there any documented or noticeable intent to focus on one type of Web page content over another. This is of course at least partly due to the fact that the engines covered here are the "general" Web search engines and we're not addressing the specialized search engines, of which there are an increasing number (see Chapter Twelve).

Update Frequency

The "currentness" of the contents of a Web search service's database is primarily dependent upon how frequently crawlers crawl known sites, how quickly the new and changed pages they find are added to the database, and how quickly "submitted URLs" are visited and added to the database.

Even within a single Web search service, these factors can change frequently. Sites currently within a search engine's database may be revisited every few weeks, but more popular sites may be visited more frequently and less popular sites less frequently.

The timespan from when a new page was submitted or crawled until it gets fully indexed ranges from a day (maybe less) to a matter of months. Various engines make various claims, with varying levels of credibility. You may be able to find a page that was added yesterday. However, be aware that it may also take weeks or months in some engines. Pages that are linked from high-profile sites have a good chance of being found more quickly than those from obscure sites.

Some services promise to get submitted sites added within a day or two, while others let you know it may be a matter of weeks. Also, just because a page has been added to the database doesn't mean that it's fully indexed—this may be done in stages, with the URL itself indexed first, then the title, and, sometimes even months later, the text of the page.

TYPICAL RETRIEVAL AND RANKING FACTORS

Once the user has entered a query, that input goes to the program that searches the engine's database to determine (1) which records should be considered as having matched the query, and (2) in what order those records should be displayed. These two functions can work rather independently or they can be essentially a single function.

The first function, the identification of records, is most typically done based on either (a) using a default approach in which the user has entered terms, phrases, or sentences without any required syntax, or (b) using input from the user that conforms to a syntax involving criteria such as Boolean operators, proximity operators, field specifiers, etc.

Tip: Bookmark your favorite search engine for direct access, rather than using the search links offered as the default when you first loaded your browser (for instance, the Netscape Search link on Netscape's Netcenter or the Microsoft default page on Internet Explorer). On any site where you see a single query box for which you can choose from a list of search engines, remember that you are most often using a dumbed-down version of some of those engines.

When the user has not used a structured syntax, the most simplistic approach for identifying the records is for the retrieval program to take all or some of the words the user entered, connect them with either a Boolean AND or OR, and search the database using that Boolean expression. With only a small degree of marketing license, this can be referred to as "natural language searching," which in a rudimentary sense it is. Those who have spent a major portion of their lives working with the tremendously sophisticated and complicated aspects of natural language processing (NLP) may be understandably annoyed when natural language terminology is used so loosely. Most search engines go beyond that rudimentary form and indeed make use of more sophisticated approaches and techniques. In most of the major engines, however, whether explicitly or otherwise, the Boolean matching is an integral part of the whole process. There are alternatives that bypass the Boolean and identify the records to be retrieved on the basis of popularity factors and sophisticated linguistic analysis involving such factors as co-occurrence of terms.

When the user makes use of a specified syntax, such as Boolean, that may even override an engine's default algorithm. By choosing to go with a syntax, the user is saying, "Thanks anyway, but I know what I'm doing and I'd prefer to take more control of the process." Some might think of the two approaches as the difference between a TV dinner and a meal prepared from scratch. The relative merits of the product depend on how good a cook one is. A single engine

Tip: If it's not documented, *guess* but don't *assume*.

If it is documented, don't necessarily assume it always works—i.e., don't assume that it was you who made the mistake if it doesn't work.

may provide all of these alternatives: a default algorithm based on implicit Boolean and other criteria, user-applied syntax, and sophisticated linguistic analysis.

With the first function of the program being the identification of "qualifying" records, the second major function of the search engine's retrieval/ranking program is to determine the relative relevance of each record. This is often expressed as a "score" or "ranking"—i.e., the program's estimate as to how well a particular record meets the intent of the query. As stated above, this can be integrated into the first function, with a record's "ranking" determining whether or not the record is retrieved (only those meeting some threshold score will be displayed in the results).

Because of the competitive nature of the search engine industry, details of the retrieval and ranking algorithms are often closely guarded. For effective use of search engines, it's useful to go into a little more detail about the factors that are involved—the things the search engine looks for in a record to determine if it should be retrieved and how it should be ranked in terms of relevance. The latter usually determines the order in which records are presented to the user. In the profiles later in this book, the "known" factors for each engine will be discussed briefly. Those interested in knowing more should examine whatever details are provided in the engine's online documentation.

The factors that go into determining whether or not the record is retrieved and the record's ranking (score) usually incorporate some combination of the following:

- Popularity of the page—How "popular" a page is has become a factor for most engines. In some engines (like Google) it's the primary factor. Popularity is usually measured in one of two ways. "Link" popularity assigns a value to a record based on how many pages link to it. "Click" popularity assigns a score to a record based on how often people have clicked on that record at other times when the user's particular query was searched.

- Frequency of terms—If a query term occurs more than once in the record, points are accrued. Greater numbers of occurrences may add additional points, but most search engines put a limit on how far this goes, in order to defeat programmers' attempts to unjustifiably increase rankings by simply repeating a word numerous (even hundreds of) times. The length of the document is sometimes also factored in, with two occurrences in a short document providing more points than two occurrences in a long document.

- Number of query terms that are matched—If your query consists of three words, those records having all three words will get more points than a record having only one or two.

- Rarity of terms—If your query has one term that's very common and a second that occurs only a few times in the search engine's database, a record containing the rare term may get a higher score than one with the common term.

- Weighting by field—If a query term occurs in the record's title, that counts for more than if it only appears later in the text.

- Proximity of terms—If two of your query terms are close together that counts for more than if they are far apart.

- Weighting according to the order in which the searcher entered terms—A record containing your first term may get more points than one containing the word you entered second.

- Word variants (and/or truncation)—Some engines can identify words that have the same root as your query term (for example, plurals). The engine may then retrieve records containing those variants as well as records containing your exact term.

- Case-sensitivity—Some engines distinguish uppercase from lowercase. In these situations, the engine can refine your search by returning only those records with an exact case match. If in your query you enter "AIDS," those engines can return only those records that have that word in all uppercase, and prevent you from having to look at lots of records about instructional aids, breathing aids, etc.

- Analysis of documents in the database—Term association, associative networks, cluster analysis, co-occurrence, and a variety of other linguistic-based approaches may be applied.
- Relevance feedback applied to retrieved records—As a second step on the user's part, in some engines you can identify a record you like and ask for "more like this one." The engine then examines records that have similar content to the record you liked.
- Date—More recent records are given more points than older records.

BENCHMARKS

To understand the differences between the search engines, it makes sense to do some specific head-on comparisons as to how much is actually retrieved by one engine versus another. In interpreting results of such comparisons, considerable caution should be applied because of the numerous variables involved, such as presence of duplicates among the results in any engine, reliability of numbers reported by the engines, constant changes in sizes of the databases and so on. The best benchmarking for search engines is probably that done by an individual comparing results for words, phrases, etc. in subject areas relevant to the individual's particular area of research. The following "benchmarks" however, which come from a variety of subject fields, should give some idea of the relative performance of the engines.

Before examining the chart that follows (Table 1.2) the reader should acknowledge some caveats. First, the numbers shown are those *reported by the service* for each search. It was not feasible to check if the numbers are actually "correct" in terms of whether each of the reported numbers represents a valid, unduplicated, still-available page. For a good analysis of these factors see Greg Notess' Search Engine Showdown at searchengineshowdown.com.

Perhaps most importantly, there is one conclusion that the reader must not draw from the chart: that one can pick the engine with the highest numbers and stick with that one engine. Each of the major engines, because of the low degree of overlap (which is discussed in greater detail in the next section), can produce a significant number

Table 1.2 Benchmarking Results

	AltaVista	Excite	Fast Search	Google	HotBot	Lycos	Northern Light (1)
aberystwyth	73,795	20,320	70,468	**158,000**	36,100	37,439	61,138
chrodegang	**422**	90	356	255	98	232	201
"alvin toffler"	6,810	635	**12,667**	12,500	10,600	9,849	9,628
"sidereal messenger"	247	246	**383**	312	157	257	256
+"red wine" +cancer +resveratrol	428	353	1,021	968	**1,100**	616	766
+crumpton +maryland +auction	27	26	53	45	40	52	**86**
(trilobite OR trilobites) AND morphology	802	639	**1,262**	--	1,200	--	1,170

(1) Web results only (not from Special Collection)

Note that the "winner" for each benchmark is indicated in bold. What can be concluded is that there's a wide variation in the retrieval of the various engines and no particular engine always comes up with the largest retrieval. The primary reasons for the differences in numbers are the size of the database, the quality of the retrieval algorithm, and the depth of indexing of the pages contained in the database. Each of these factors also contributes to the fact that, for a typical question, each of the larger engines will retrieve records missed by the other large engines.

of results not found by its "competitors." Even the smaller engines often retrieve some records not retrieved by the larger engines. Using only one search engine in most cases will deprive the searcher of these relevant records.

OVERLAP OF RETRIEVAL BETWEEN ENGINES

One of the most important points that can be made about using Web search engines effectively is the following: **If you're interested in good recall (finding most of the sites that match your needs) you MUST consider searching more than one search engine.**

This is not to say that you *always* need to search more than one engine. If you're looking for a specific page, or a specific piece of information and you find it in the first engine you search, wonderful!

However, if you're looking for background material, if you're not sure exactly what it is you're after, if you look at the results from one engine and aren't sure you have found the best answer or the full answer, **you MUST consider searching more than one search engine.**

This can be brought home by an example. Five search engines were searched for the phrase "erris head." The following were the numbers of distinct records that were retrieved by each:

Fast Search	45
Northern Light	36
AltaVista	31
Excite	16
HotBot	9

At first glance there may seem to be a clear "winner." However, an analysis of the individual records showed that there were a total of 64 unique records. Among these 64 records:

- The highest-retrieving engine found only 70 percent
- The second-highest-retrieving engine found 12 that weren't in the first.

- The top two together still missed 7 records (over 10 percent)
- Excite and HotBot, the two with the lowest numbers, together found 7 records that the top three missed.

This is just one example, but similar testing using other words produces approximately comparable results.

CHAPTER 2

Common Searching Options

With some understanding now of where search engines come from and how they're put together, the next step toward effective usage is a more detailed understanding of the searching features they provide. These features typically include options to search only selected portions of the database, Boolean logic, truncation, phrase searching, proximity searching, proper name searching, field searching, and your choice of output format and number of records to appear on each results page. A variety of other features are provided by individual search engines and will be discussed in the chapters profiling them. By looking at the more common features at a general level here, it will be easier to understand and use them as they are presented by any particular engine.

SELECTION OF WHAT IS TO BE SEARCHED

When using search engines that have an accompanying directory, you may be given a choice to either search the entire database or just the sites that are included in the directory. Some search engine databases actually comprise different collections of documents. With Northern Light, for instance, you're given the option of searching Web documents, Northern Light's collection of proprietary documents, or both. You may also be given choices of searching Usenet, e-mail directories, or other options.

When you choose to search other than "the Web," you will in many cases be transferring to an interface that is significantly different from the interface for searching the Web. The search engine service may attempt to make such an interface look like its own as much as possible, but because of differences in the types of information covered it may out of necessity look quite different.

BOOLEAN LOGIC

Boolean (or Boolean logic, Boolean algebra, etc.) for our purposes here, can be described as the use of operators such as AND, OR, and NOT, to identify those pages (records) that contain a specific combination of terms.

All major search engines offer some form of Boolean searching, either "simplified Boolean" (using pluses and minuses) or "full" Boolean (AND, OR, NOT).

If a search engine has full Boolean capabilities, it will offer the following search options or the equivalents of each:

AND—To specify that both words must be present. For instance:

> automobile AND sales

would retrieve only those pages where both the word "automobile" and the word "sales" are present on the same page (same record).

OR—To specify that either word can be present. For instance:

> automobile OR car

would retrieve all of those pages (records) that have the word "automobile" plus all of those pages (records) that have the word "car."

NOT—To exclude a word. For instance:

> automobile NOT van

would retrieve all those pages (records) that have the word "automobile" except those that have the word "van." All those with "van" would be excluded.

Nesting Capabilities (using parentheses)—To indicate how the words are grouped together, or the order in which the parts of the Boolean statement should be executed. For instance:

(automobile OR car) AND sales

would retrieve all the records that have the word "sales" and also have either the word "automobile" or "car." Note that the same effect would not necessarily result if the parentheses are omitted.

Some engines have simplified Boolean, offering one or more but not all of the above functions (usually AND in the form of +word and NOT in the form of -word). The most commonly missing feature is the nesting capability. Without this capability, more complicated Boolean queries—especially those involving multiple groupings of OR terms—cannot necessarily be accomplished.

A typical expression using the full range of Boolean functions would be:

"chemical industry" AND (Mexico OR Mexican) NOT pollution

Table 2.1 illustrates how the above search phrase would be expressed or approximated in each of the major search engines (for engines with more than one version, the version shown is the one that provides the greatest Boolean capability). For engines such as Fast Search and Lycos that do not have full Boolean and do not necessarily AND all terms together, there's a way to closely approximate a Boolean search that contains one set of ORs, as in the example above. Enter ANDed terms with pluses, NOTed terms with the minus and the ORed terms with neither. In the Lycos example above, this will indeed get you lots of records that don't mention Mexico or Mexican, but the ones that *do* have those terms should appear close to the top of the list because of relevance ranking. In other words, +A B C -D approximately equals A AND (B OR C) NOT D.

Be aware that use of Boolean operators in the form of AND, OR, NOT, and AND NOT will sometimes override the relevance retrieval (+word and -word usually do not). If all you need to do is AND words

Table 2.1 Comparison of Boolean statements in different search engines

Search Engine	Full Boolean?	Expression
AltaVista (Advanced)	yes	"chemical industry" AND (Mexico OR Mexican) AND NOT pollution
Excite (Basic)	yes	"chemical industry" AND (Mexico OR Mexican) NOT pollution
Fast Search	almost	+"chemical industry" +(Mexico Mexican) -pollution (first choose "any of the words" in the pull-down window)
Google	almost	"chemical industry" Mexico OR Mexican -pollution
HotBot	yes	"chemical industry" AND (Mexico OR Mexican) NOT pollution (Be sure to choose "Boolean phrase" in the "Search for" window.)
Lycos Advanced	no	+"chemical industry" Mexico Mexican -pollution (first choose "any words" in the pull-down window)
Northern Light	yes	"chemical industry" AND (Mexico OR Mexican) NOT pollution
Yahoo!	no	+"chemical industry" +Mexic* -pollution [asterisk is for truncating for "Mexico" or "Mexican." See below.]

together, stick to the pluses and minuses—it's easy to understand and to enter, and you run less risk of overriding relevance ranking.

Regarding capitalization of Boolean operators, some engines require that they be capitalized, others do not. The simplest approach for the searcher is to always capitalize them. This way you're safe and also don't have to worry about knowing whether capitalization is required in a particular engine.

TRUNCATION

Truncation, the facility for searching on the stem or root of a word, is a feature available in most, but not all, of the major search engines. You'll often see this feature referred to as "wildcards." In some engines, truncation is automatic and the search engine automatically recognizes and retrieves words with variant endings. In others, the user specifies that truncation should take place by ending the stem of the word with a truncation symbol (usually an asterisk).

This can greatly simplify searching for terms that can have a variety of suffixes (-s, -ing, -ed, -ology -ological, -ness, -ful, etc.) as well as automatically pick up some relevant compound words.

Tip: If you're in a hurry and don't want to bother checking to see if the search engine uses Boolean, go ahead and use either the pluses and minuses or AND and OR. For the latter, chances are that if the engine doesn't use them it will ignore the words.

PHRASE AND PROXIMITY SEARCHING

Search engines may allow the user to specify how close two words should be to each other. This may take the form of "phrase searching" where a precise phrase of two or more words can be entered and that exact phrase searched. This is most commonly accomplished by entering the phrase with double quotation marks around it. Some services allow additional flexibility with the NEAR or similar operators.

The NEAR operator allows for two words to be a certain distance apart, sometimes allowing the searcher to specify the maximum distance. In AltaVista, for example, *medical NEAR malpractice* would find records that contain both words no farther than 10 words apart. The NEAR operator is an excellent way to get high precision yet allow for the numerous ways a writer may address the concept. See the Search Engines Features Guide (Table 2.4) beginning on page 51, and the individual search engine profiles for details about each engine. As of this writing, AltaVista is the only engine discussed in this book that provides the NEAR function.

Table 2.2 Truncation Features in Different Search Engines

	Automatic or User-Controlled	Truncation Symbol	Example(s)	Special Notes
AltaVista	User-Controlled	*	horse* lab*r	Minimum three characters Will match from 0-5 lowercase additional characters. Internal truncation allowed
Excite	Automatic		horse mouse	"Concept-based retrieval" approximates automatic truncation
HotBot	User-Controlled	term* (asterisk)	horse* engineer?	Works erratically
Northern Light	User-Controlled	Automatic plural/singular * (for endings or internal) % (for single character)	horse* workm%n	Minimum four leading characters
Yahoo!	User-Controlled	*	manufact*	Some automatic truncation also takes place

NAME SEARCHING

To be able to search specifically for "names" of companies and people is something that some search engines can accomplish "approximately" by virtue of an ability to distinguish between uppercase and lowercase. When these engines receive a query in which the first letters of the words are capitalized, they assume it may be a proper name. An engine may also, when you specify that you want to search for a name, automatically allow for the inverted form of the name—that is, find *Churchill, Winston* as well as *Winston Churchill.*

The engines have no magical way of knowing whether what you enter is indeed a "name." In one engine, for example, when specifying a search for "the person," the engine found over 1,000 pages with the alleged "person" named "Frank Discussion." (Frank: If you're really out there, my sincerest apologies for doubting your existence. I hope it will cause no long-lasting identity crisis.)

FIELD SEARCHING—SEARCHING WITHIN SPECIFIC PARTS OF A RECORD

"Field searching" refers to the capability of specifying that your search be limited to a particular part or parts of the records. When this capability is present, it offers a means of easily achieving much greater precision. For example, limiting to the title field can quickly narrow a search down to only those records that so

Name Searching Tips

- Capitalize names appropriately, so you can copy and paste the name effectively from one engine to another.
- If an engine uses full Boolean but doesn't have the **NEAR** operator,
    Put the name in double quotes " "
    Enter all the possible variants ORed together

  Example:
  "Dwight Eisenhower" OR "Dwight David Eisenhower" OR
  "Dwight D Eisenhower" OR "Eisenhower, Dwight"

  The above example will work in:
    AltaVista—Power, Advanced
    HotBot (*choose* **"the Boolean phrase"** *in the* **"Look for"** *box*)
    Excite (*a lot of irrelevant ones will also be retrieved*)
    Northern Light

  Because of the number of records on someone like Eisenhower, you may want to combine the above with further qualifications.

- If the engine provides the NEAR operator, use it if you expect the possibility of middle names and or initials (AltaVista—Advanced). This will allow for the name to be inverted and will also allow for middle names. For example, in AltaVista,

  Franklin NEAR Roosevelt will retrieve:
    Franklin Roosevelt
    Franklin Delano Roosevelt
    Franklin D. Roosevelt
    Roosevelt, Franklin
    Franklin and Eleanor Roosevelt

directly address the topic that the topic was included in the title of the page. By searching within the URL field, you can quickly limit your retrieval to just those records from a particular organization, or even part of an organization.

Compared to traditional online searching (DIALOG, LEXIS-NEXIS, STN, etc.), field searching with Web search engines is fairly rudimentary. Most engines provide only a half-dozen or so searchable fields compared to 20 to over 200 with "old-time" online services. Searchable fields are summarized in Table 2.3.

The following are some of the more useful and frequently encountered fields:

Title

This is definitely a field that most searchers should frequently take advantage of. It provides a quick and easy way to get your hands on what are very often the most relevant records. Be very aware, though, that you use this at the risk of losing some other very relevant records where your query concept was emphasized, but not included in the title. For instance, the *perfect* recipe for okra may be found in a record entitled "World's Best Recipes for Slimy Vegetables."

Also be aware that a page's "Title" is the word or phrase that appears in the banner at the very top of your browser's window (unless you have some off-brand browser, which you may not want to admit to). The "title" may not be what, by looking at the page's content, you think would be the title.

Some engines allow searching of only single words in the title, others allow an entire phrase. In Table 2.3, where the example shows a phrase it means that phrases in a title are searchable in that engine. If only a single-word example is given, it indicates that the engine does not effectively search title *phrases*.

Date

Keep in mind that "Date" in Web search engines refers not necessarily to the "publication date" of the material included on the page but usually to (a) the creation date given in the page's HTML, (b) the "last modified" date for the page, or (c) the date the search engine found or last checked the page.

URL

This field is most useful when you want to limit your retrieval to pages from a particular organization. It will often be used in conjunction with other search terms. For example, a search on "vasculitis AND url:jhu.edu" would retrieve only records from Johns Hopkins University that mention vasculitis. (If a Web search engine has indexed a site completely, and the site itself does not provide a search capability, you can in effect use this approach as a search engine for that particular site.)

URLs are searched to varying degrees of detail and with varying approaches. In some cases you can distinguish between domain, host, and overall URL—for example, *url:gov, url:irs.gov, url: procurement.irs.gov.* Most search engines are very flexible here, allowing you to search any contiguous segments of the URL, including directories and file names to the right of the domain portion of the URL. In HotBot, "continent" is a derivation of URL country domain names, bringing together all those country codes for each continent.

Images and Other Media

Finding pages that contain images is handled very differently by different engines. The different approaches can make a big difference in whether you find the image you wish. Some engines, such as AltaVista and Lycos, provide completely separate media-searching options that don't require you to do a "field" search, since those options only search media, not the Web in general. In HotBot, you can specify your subject, such as "ostrich," in the query box and then specify that you only want pages that contain images. You'll probably find many of the pages that have an image of an ostrich, but you'll also get pages mentioning ostrich in the text but that have images completely unrelated to the bird (including company logos, word images used as directory buttons, and other kinds of images).

Other Page Content

Other content is handled in a variety of ways related to the types of files and programming that are included in a page. Many, such as applets and objects, are mostly of interest to programmers or Web page designers looking at how specific devices are handled or used.

Links

The capability of searching for links is a potentially very powerful device but useful only for a fairly small portion of searches. When searching the "links" field (in AltaVista, Fast Search, Google, HotBot, and Lycos), this feature allows you to find pages that link to the URL (or portion of a URL) you specify. Try it out on your own organization's URL (or a page within your organization's site) to see who's linking to you. Link, or "link-to," searching is parallel to the citation searching pioneered commercially by Eugene Garfield (of

Image Saving Tips

To save an image that you've located, hold your cursor over the image and click your right mouse button (on a Mac, hold down your mouse button for a second or so). A menu will pop up. Choose the "Save image as" option, then choose the location to save it in, name the file, and click "Save." You can change the name of the file, but don't change the file extension (.gif, .jpg, .jpeg, etc.).

the Institute for Scientific Information) in the 1960s with Science Citation Index and the other ISI citation indexes—with some of the same advantages. If you're looking for an obscure or hard-to-define topic, and you've located one relevant page, it could be useful to identify other pages that link to the page you've found. If you're tracking a small company, it might be useful to see who's linking to that company's page. When using this option you may need to try searching several variations of the URL, such as onstrat.com, www.onstrat.com, and, in some cases, http://www.onstrat.com.

Date Searching—Special Consideration

Be aware that within Web search engines, "date" usually does not refer to the date of publication of the content of a Web page, but rather to the date when the page was created or last modified. If no creation or "last modified" date is on the page, the engine may use the date the page was picked up by the search engine.

"MORE LIKE THIS ONE"

As a second step on the user's part, in some engines you can identify a record you like and ask for "more like this one." The engine then selects and returns records that have similar content to the record you liked.

OUTPUT OPTIONS

In reporting an answer, most engines tell you how many records were retrieved. They may also give the counts for each individual term if the query contained more than one term.

Some engines provide alternate format options that may include a short one with just URL or title, a medium format including a few other elements, and a more detailed format that includes a summary of the page or the first few words of the page (typically Title, URL, Summary, etc.). The long format is usually the default.

Table 2.3 Field Searching Using Different Search Engines

ENGINE	FIELD	SEARCHED FROM	PREFIX/ SYNTAX	EXAMPLE(S)
AltaVista Letter indicates the mode in which the field is available: **H=Home P=Power A=Advanced R=Raging Search**	*Using Prefixes:* Title	Query box	title:	title:"San Jose Mercury"
	URL - Domain host URL	" " " " " "	domain: host: url:	domain:uk host:faxon.com url:whale.simmons url:whale.simmons.edu url:simmons.edu/archives
	anchor	" "	anchor:	anchor:contact
	applet	" "	applet:	applet:class
	image	" "	image:	image:reindeer
	like	" "	like:	like:viking.no
	link	" "	link:	link:adlittle
	object	" "	object:	object:marquee
	text	" "	text:	text:Marblehead
	Using windows, boxes, etc.:			
	title	"Search by" window	(choose "Title…")	"European Union"
	date	(P,A,R) Date range boxes	dd/mm/yr	30/11/99 to 10/06/00
	language	Language window (H,P,A,R)	("choose from list")	French
	link	"Search by" window (P) "that link to…" box (R)	(choose "Links to") (text box)	adlittle www.onstrat.com
	continent	"by region" window (P)	("choose from list")	Asia
	URL (URL, domain, host)	"by domain," "by URL or host" boxes (P,R)	(window, text box) (text box)	www.merck.com

ENGINE	FIELD	SEARCHED FROM	PREFIX/ SYNTAX	EXAMPLE(S)
AltaVista (*cont.*)	anchor	"…in the anchor" box (R)	(text box)	reservation
	image	"…image" box (R)		kierkegaard
Excite (Advanced)	language	Language window	(choose from list)	Dutch
	country	Country/Domain window	"	Italy
	domain type	" " "	"	.com
Fast Search (Advanced)	language	Language window	(choose from list)	German
	title	Word Filter window	(text box)	"borgia family"
	URL	Word Filter window and Domain Filters window (latter for top-level domain and specific Web site only)	(text box)	.edu simmons.edu whale.simmons.edu simmons.edu/archives
	link	Word Filter window	(text box)	onstrat.com
	link name (anchor)	Word Filter window	(text box)	"contact us"
Google Letter indicates the mode in which the field is available: **H=Home A=Advanced**	title	Query box (H) Occurence box (A)	allintitle:	allintitle: "online strategies" online strategies
	URL	Query box (H) Occurence box (A)	url:	url:temple.edu ox.ac.uk
	site	Query box (H) Domains box (A)	site:	physics site:cam.ac.uk
	language	language window (A)	(choose from list)	Deutsch Japanese
	link	"Find pages that link…" box (A)	link: (text box)	link:fas.org fas.org

Table 2.3 Field Searching Using Different Search Engines (*cont.*)

Table 2.3 Field Searching Using Different Search Engines (*cont.*)

ENGINE	FIELD	SEARCHED FROM	PREFIX/ SYNTAX	EXAMPLE(S)
HotBot (A) [indicates only available in Advanced Search]	*Using Window Choices:* title	"Look for" box	(choose "the page title" then use text box)	ostrich leather
	URL	(A)Location panel		uk faxon.com edu simmons.edu artemis.simmons.edu
	date	Date window (A)Date panel	(choose from list) (choose from list)	*In the last week* [*after* or *before* date selected from list]
	region	(A)Location panel	(choose from list)	Europe North America (.com)
	media type	"Pages Must Include" panel	(check boxes)	Image Audio
	file extension		(check box)	.gif
	page depth		radio buttons	Top page
	Using Prefixes: title	Query Box	title:	title:stearate
	domain	Query Box	domain:	domain:org domain:ipl.org domain:hypatia.ipl.org
	page depth	Query Box	depth:	depth:3
	feature	Query Box	feature:	feature:video feature:applet feature:image feature:audio
Lycos (all of these apply only to the Advanced page)	title	"Page Field" tab Query Box	(text box) t:	"search engines" t:"wooden bridges"
	URL- URL Host/Domain	"Page Field" tab " " "	" " " " "	ancestry.com .uk

Table 2.3 Field Searching Using Different Search Engines (*cont.*)

ENGINE	FIELD	SEARCHED FROM	PREFIX/ SYNTAX	EXAMPLE(S)
Lycos **(cont.)**	URL-(cont.)			cam.ac eng.cam.ac.uk
		Query box	u:	u:bayer.de
	language	Language tab Query box	(choose from list) l:	Catalan l:fre
	media/ document type	Content tab	radio buttons	Multimedia Books
	link	Link Referrals tab Query box	(text boxes) ml:	linde.de ml:madeira.org
Northern Light Letter indicates search page in which the field is available: **(H) = Home** **(P) = Power** **(B) = Business** **(I) = Investext** **(S) = Stocks** **(N) = News** **(G) = GeoSearch**	*Using Prefixes in main or "Search for" query box:* **URL** (H)(P)(B)(G)	Query box	url:	url:whale:simmons url:whale:simmons.edu url:simmons.edu/archives
	title (H)(P)(B)(I)(N)(G)	Query box	title:	title:parliament title:"online strategies"
	publication (H)(P)(B)(N)	Query box	pub:	pub:"africa news service"
	company (H)(P)(B)(I)(N)(G)	Query box	company:	company:"General Motors"
	ticker (H)(P)(B)(I)(N)(G)	Query box " "	ticker: (text box)	ticker:bur bur
	text (H)(P)(B)(I)(N)(G)	Query box	text:	text:apparel
	Using field-specific query boxes, check boxes, etc.: **URL** (P)	"Words in URL" box	(text box)	whale:simmons whale:simmons.edu simmons.edu/archives
	title (P)(B)(I)	"Words in title" box	(text box)	"field searching" "online strategies"

Table 2.3 Field Searching Using Different Search Engines (*cont.*)

ENGINE	FIELD	SEARCHED FROM	PREFIX/ SYNTAX	EXAMPLE(S)
Northern Light *(cont.)*	**publication** (P)(B)(G)	"Publication name" box	(text box)	"Agricultural History"
	subject category (P)(G)	"Limit subjects to" check boxes	(check boxes)	Health & Medicine
	document type (P)(B)(I)(G)	"Limit documents to" check boxes	(check boxes)	press releases
	language (P)(B)(I)	Language window	(choose from list)	German
	country (P)	"Web sites from" window	(choose from list)	Australia
	date (P)(B)(I)(G)	Date range boxes	mm/dd/yyyy	12/21/1999
	company name (B)(I)(G)	"Company name" text box	(text box)	Bayer
	industry (B)(I)	"Limit industry to" check boxes	(check boxes)	Hospitality
	research firm (B)(I)	"Research firm" text box	(text box)	williams de broe
	ticker symbol (S)	query box	(text box)	ibm
	document length (I)	"Limit by length of document" check boxes	(check boxes)	Medium
	region (I)	"region" checkboxes	(check boxes)	Europe
	location	text boxes	(text boxes)	22181
Yahoo!	**title**	Query box	t: or title:	t:molecular magnetism
	URL	" "	u: or url:	u:infonortics

Image Searching Tips

There are basically two ways to search for images using Web search engines. You can either take advantage of special image databases provided by some services or you can search the service's regular Web database and indicate that you want an image. The former usually works far better and is easier. Whether you're looking for an image of a person, place, thing, or whatever, these engines can probably lead you to it.

AltaVista, Lycos, and Fast Search provide large image databases.

•In AltaVista, click on the "Images" link on the home page, then enter your search terms in the query box. (You can use virtually all of the search features available on AltaVista's home page, such as +, -, and various prefixes such as "title:".) Keep in mind that the descriptions attached to images are usually fairly brief, so don't add too many qualifications. Using radio buttons and a window, you can also specify whether you want photos, graphics, black and white, color, or buttons/banners. You can also choose which image collection you want searched. AltaVista will return thumbnail images from which to select.

•With Lycos, click on the Multimedia link on the home page (under the query box). Enter your topic in the query box. Choose All, Pictures, Audio, or Video, and then click the "search" button. You can search using simple Boolean (+term, -term) and quotation marks for phrases. Lycos provides a section on the Multimedia page for downloading a wide range of media applications files for use with the search results.

•Fast Search actually produces the image-search technology used by Lycos, and Fast Search itself provides more image-search options. With Fast Search, click on the multimedia link on the home page. On the resulting page, choose "images" from the pull-down window and enter your term(s). On the results page you are given options to narrow down your search by specifying your choice of image format type, transparency, color, grey, or line art. From the first Multimedia page you can also get these options by clicking on Advanced Search.

General Searching Tips

1. Think about your strategy before picking your engine.
2. Decide what features would be helpful:
   - Boolean logic?
   - parentheses?
   - proximity?
   - truncation?
   - phrases?
3. Find out which engines provide those features (use Table 2.4—Search Engines Features Guide).
4. Start *specific*, then move *broader* as needed. Get a feel for what's there, then modify your strategy appropriately.
5. Don't hesitate to try several engines and different approaches. Remember you're not paying for connect time.
6. Try at least two engines unless the first one gives you just what you need. If you're looking for a specific fact or a specific page, use one search engine after the other until you find it or decide it's time to give up. If you're looking for "background" and are not sure what you might want, ALWAYS use at least two search engines.
7. For searching across several engines:
   - Use copy and paste to save and re-use your query (on PCs: Control-C, Control-V; on Macintoshes: the ⌘-C, ⌘-V keys).
   - When using operators, use uppercase characters. For any engine that uses the Boolean operators, uppercase will work. Lowercase will work with some, but not others. By sticking to uppercase, you don't need to worry about which to use.
   - When searching for names, capitalize to make the query more workable across engines.

The engines typically display 10 records per page as the default, while some engines give you options for larger increments—in some cases up to 100 per page.

INTERNATIONAL VERSIONS

Several search engines provide country-specific or region-specific versions and also non-English interfaces. The links to these

Table 2.4 Search Engines Features Guide

	AltaVista Home www.altavista.com	AltaVista Advanced	Excite Home www.excite.com	Excite Advanced Search
SIZE (pages)	700 million	700 million	250 million	250 million
SIMPLE BOOLEAN	+term -term defaults to an AND		+term -term defaults to an OR	(menu)
FULL BOOLEAN		OR AND AND NOT ( )	OR AND NOT ( )	
PHRASE	" "	" "	" "	(menu)
PROXIMITY		NEAR (=within 10 words)		
TRUNCATION	term* (asterisk)	term* (asterisk)	automatic	automatic
TITLE FIELD		title:term		
DATE FIELD		(date range boxes)		
URL FIELD	url:term domain:term host:term	url:term domain:term host:term		(menu, domain only)
"LINKS TO" A URL	link:term	link:term		
LANGUAGE	(menu)	(menu)		(menu)
MEDIA SEARCHING	media search tabs	media search tabs		yes
CASE SENSITIVE	yes	yes		
SEARCHES ALL COMMON WORDS	yes	yes		
WEB DIRECTORY ATTACHED	yes LookSmart	yes LookSmart	yes	
GIVES COUNT FOR ANSWER	yes	yes		
OUTPUT OPTIONS	Customizable 10, 20, 30, 40, 50 results per page	Customizable 10, 20, 30, 40, 50 results per page	Titles Titles & summaries Grouped/ungrouped by Web site	10,20,30,50 results Titles Titles & summaries Grouped/ungrouped by Web site
ALSO SHOWN ON RESULTS PAGES	RealNames Related searches Directory hits "Related pages" "More pages from this site" Link to factsheets	Link to "More pages from this site" Link to factsheets	Stock quotes Sports scores Weather Company information News, etc.	
"MORE LIKE THIS"	yes	yes		
OUTSTANDING SPECIAL FEATURES	Images/audio/video search Translations Adult content filter Hit terms highlighted	Images/audio/video search Translations Adult content filter Hit terms highlighted	News Tracker	Search by country

Table 2.4 Search Engines Features Guide *(cont.)*

	Fast Search Home www.alltheweb.com	Fast Search Advanced	Google www.google.com
SIZE (pages)	575 million	575 million	575+ million fully indexed 500+ million partially indexed
SIMPLE BOOLEAN	(menu) +term -term defaults to an AND (term1 term2)	(menu) +term -term defaults to an AND	-term defaults to an AND
FULL BOOLEAN			OR
PHRASE	(menu) " "	(menu) " "	" "
PROXIMITY			
TRUNCATION			
TITLE FIELD		(menu)	allintitle:
DATE FIELD			
URL FIELD		(menu) (domain filters box)	allinurl:
"LINKS TO" A URL		(menu) (word filter box)	link:term
LANGUAGE		(menu) (word filter box)	(menu-Advanced)
MEDIA SEARCHING	Link to media searches (via Lycos)	(via Lycos)	
CASE SENSITIVE			
SEARCHES ALL COMMON WORDS	yes	yes	
WEB DIRECTORY ATTACHED			yes Open Directory
GIVES COUNT FOR ANSWER	yes	yes	yes
OUTPUT OPTIONS	Standard	Standard 10, 25, 50, 75, 100	10, 20, 30, 50, 100 results
ALSO SHOWN ON RESULTS PAGES			RealNames Link to cached page Definitions Directory links
"MORE LIKE THIS"			yes
OUTSTANDING SPECIAL FEATURES	FTP search (Lycos) Image Search	Adult-content filter Image Search FTP Search (Lycos)	Retrieval based on "link" popularity Cached pages Hit terms highlighted

Table 2.4 Search Engines Features Guide *(cont.)*

	HotBot Home www.hotbot.com	HotBot Advanced	Lycos Home www.lycos.com	Lycos Advanced
SIZE (pages)	500 million	500 million	575 million	575 million
SIMPLE BOOLEAN	(menu) +term -term defaults to an AND	(menu) +term -term defaults to an AND	+term -term defaults to an AND	(menu) +term -term defaults to an AND
FULL BOOLEAN	OR AND NOT ( ) (must also use menu)	OR AND NOT ( ) (must also use menu)		AND OR NOT ( )
PHRASE	(menu) " "	(menu) " "	" "	(menu) " "
PROXIMITY				
TRUNCATION	term* (asterisk)	term* (asterisk)		
TITLE FIELD	(menu) title:term	(menu) title:term		(box, under "Page Field" tab)
DATE FIELD	(menu)	(menus)		
URL FIELD	domain:term	(menus) domain:term		(boxes, under "Page Field" tab)
"LINKS TO" A URL	(menu)	(menu)		(boxes, under "Link Referrals" tab)
LANGUAGE	(menu)	(menu)		(radio buttons, under "Language" tab)
MEDIA SEARCHING	(check boxes)	(check boxes)	Link to "Multimedia Search"	(radio button)
CASE SENSITIVE	sometimes	sometimes		
SEARCHES ALL COMMON WORDS				
WEB DIRECTORY ATTACHED	yes Open Directory		yes	(link to Open Directory)
GIVES COUNT FOR ANSWER	approximate	approximate	yes	yes
OUTPUT OPTIONS	Full, brief URLs only 10, 25, 50, 100 results Results from this site only	Full, brief URLs only 10, 25, 50, 100 results Results from this site only	standard	standard
ALSO SHOWN ON RESULTS PAGES	Related searches Direct Hit popularity results (top 10) Directory hits	Related searches Direct Hit popularity results (first 10) Directory hits	Popularity results. Directory hits. Links to company profiles, home pages, quotes, news, etc. Matching news and shopping items	
"MORE LIKE THIS"	yes	yes		
OUTSTANDING SPECIAL FEATURES	Direct Hit popularity results	Direct Hit popularity results. Search by region	Adult content filter Hit terms highlighted	Adult-content filter Additional databases for down-loads, MP3, news, etc. /Hit terms highlighted

Table 2.4 Search Engines Features Guide *(cont.)*

	Northern Light Home www.northernlight.com	Northern Light Power Search	Yahoo! www.yahoo.com
SIZE (pages)	360 million	360 million	1-2 million (est.) in directory, 1 billion from Google
SIMPLE BOOLEAN	-term +term defaults to AND	+term -term defaults to AND	+term -term defaults to AND
FULL BOOLEAN	OR AND NOT ( )	OR AND NOT ( )	
PHRASE	" "	" "	" "
PROXIMITY			
TRUNCATION	automatic plural/sing. term* (asterisk - internal or at end of term) % (for single char.)	automatic plural/sing. term* (asterisk - internal or at end of term) % (for single char.)	Automatic term* (asterisk)
TITLE FIELD	title:term	("Words in title" box) title:term	t:term title:term
DATE FIELD		(date range boxes)	(menu under "Advanced Search")
URL FIELD	url:term	("Words in URL box) url:term	u:term url:term
"LINKS TO" A URL			
LANGUAGE		(language menu)	
MEDIA SEARCHING			
CASE SENSITIVE	Exact matches displayed first	Exact matches displayed first	
SEARCHES ALL COMMON WORDS	yes	yes	
WEB DIRECTORY ATTACHED	yes	yes	Primarily is a directory
GIVES COUNT FOR ANSWER	yes	yes	yes
OUTPUT OPTIONS	standard	standard Sort by date or relevance	Standard (Advanced Search allows choice of 10, 20, 50, 100)
ALSO SHOWN ON RESULTS PAGES	Custom Search Folders Link to "more results from this site"	Custom Search Folders Link to "more results from this site"	Categories, directory hits Google hits, news, Web events Links to company quotes, news, etc. Related searches
"MORE LIKE THIS"			
OUTSTANDING SPECIAL FEATURES	Also searches collection of non-Web publications Can narrow a search by means of folders. Link to special search forms for business, stocks, news, and Investext	Also searches collection of non-Web publications Limit to subject, document type, country Can narrow a search by means of folders Link to special search forms for business, stocks, news, Investext, GeoSearch	Hit terms highlighted Also uses Google database and news database

are generally found at the bottom of the home page. In some cases these interfaces can amount to only a translation of the search page into the other language, but usually they also provide local content not found in the main version. Some services, particularly AltaVista and Google, provide extensive help screens with explanations of how best to search using non-English vocabulary and character sets.

ABOUT THE PROFILES

As stated in the introduction, Chapters Three through Ten feature profiles of those search engines that might be considered to be the leading engines in terms of both popularity and searching capabilities. Each profile is designed to allow the searcher to easily know what the engine has to offer and how to take advantage of it. While a major goal was consistency, the unique structure of some of the engines meant that consistency sometimes had to be sacrificed in favor of clarity and completeness.

Most of the facts included in the profiles come from examining the engine's online documentation, then testing to see if that is really what happens. Usually the claims of the documentation were confirmed— in a few cases they weren't. Where the documentation didn't provide desired information, experimentation was called upon. Some information came directly from the search engine providers through other means, such as press releases and direct contact. An effort is made here to present options and syntax that seem to work (at least most of the time). When it wasn't clear that a feature was consistently working, I tended to include it in the expectation that it would be fixed soon. When using search engines be a skeptical optimist: Be willing to try any of the features, but recognize that you may not get everything the feature claims to deliver.

PORTAL FEATURES

Recognizing that the searching feature itself is a "portal" feature, we'll use the term "portal features" to describe those that involve other than searching. The *major* ones for each engine are listed and/or discussed. No attempt is made to be exhaustive for two reasons: (1) The focus of this book is primarily on the "searching" capabilities of the engines rather than on the sometimes fairly extraneous added features that do not relate directly to the searching of the engine's Web database, and (2) these features come and go on a much more frequent basis than the searching features, making information about them rather volatile. The one type of portal feature that will be discussed in some detail is directories. Though Yahoo! is primarily a directory rather than a search engine, it is given a chapter, partly because of its integration of directory and search engine capabilities, and partly because its directory nature serves as a good contrast to the other services.

Keeping up with changes in search engines will be discussed in Chapter Twelve, and updated information is available on the Web at www.extremesearcher.com.

CHAPTER 3

AltaVista
www.altavista.com or www.av.com

OVERVIEW

AltaVista combines a broad range of searching capabilities and one of the larger Web databases. For the serious searcher, it provides outstanding opportunities, but also significant complexity. Both are a result of the wide variety of content and the variety of interfaces that AltaVista presents. AltaVista users have a choice of four interfaces for its Web database: Search Home, Power Search, Advanced Search, and the very customizable Raging Search. Search features include Boolean, proximity (NEAR), and extensive field searching (plus truncation). It also offers image, audio, video, news, business, and product databases, as well as the LookSmart directory. Its

Strengths 👍	Weaknesses 👎
• Broad range of search functionality • One of the larger Web databases • Case-sensitive • Truncation (limited) • Extensive field searching • NEAR operator • Large, easy-to-use image database • Translates between English and six other languages • Matching search terms highlighted	• The variety of search interfaces, plus AltaVista's frequent urge for a "new look," can inhibit familiarity and cause confusion. • Full Boolean with ranking only available in Advanced mode • Some weaknesses in the retrieval program can cause records to be missed. • Maximum of 200 records displayed

strong image search capability and features, such as translation and customization, help contribute to its well-deserved popularity. AltaVista has indexed about 700 million Web pages.

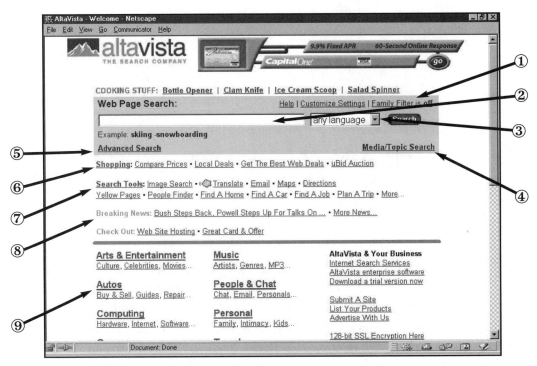

Figure 3.1 AltaVista's home (Search Home) page

Main Features on AltaVista's Home Page

① **Help**, **Family Filter**, and **Customize settings [results]** options

② **Query box**—Can use simple Boolean (+term, -term) and field prefixes (title:term, etc.)

③ **Language** option (limits results only to pages in a specific language)

④ Link to **Media/Topic** searches (Images, MP3/Audio, and Video—plus the directory, product, and news searches)

⑤ Link to **Advanced Search**—For use of full Boolean

⑥ Links to **shopping** directory, auction, etc.

⑦ Links to "**Search Tools**"—Translate, a variety of portal features, etc.

⑧   **Breaking News**—News headlines

⑨   **Directory** (LookSmart)

ALTAVISTA'S HOME PAGE

AltaVista's home page contains a query box, a number of now de-emphasized portal features, links to special searches for media (images, audio, etc.), and a link to the Advanced Search page, and, of course, shopping. AltaVista dramatically rearranges the page frequently, so be aware that the location of features will change. The query box holds virtually the same searching power as the other modes, but, other than for the language option, you need to know syntax in order to deploy the features (to search by URL, by title, etc.). You'll need to use prefixes, and you need to know that if you want Boolean, you use only simple Boolean (+term, -term). You cannot do date-range searching in Search Home.

Only one result per Web site will be shown; others are reachable by using the "More Pages from This Site" link.

WHAT HAPPENS BEHIND THE SCENES

Every day, AltaVista visits thousand of sites submitted by users, crawling over 10 million pages in the process. Every few months it performs a major crawl to rebuild its index. For every new or modified site it finds, it indexes all the words on the page, plus additional data, such as from image file names. The text in the "Description" metatag is used as an abstract and is what appears in search results to describe the page. If there is no Description metatag, the first few words of text from the page are used instead.

During indexing, AltaVista uses a technology that converts documents into Unicode, a standard encoding that allows the system to deal with most of the world's languages and character sets. Most significantly, this allows pages in non-Roman alphabets to be effectively indexed and retrieved.

AltaVista first searches to find "matches," then "ranks" them for output.

If only a string of terms is entered in Search Home or Power Search, AltaVista will usually AND all of the terms and deliver them in the order determined by the ranking algorithm. In Advanced Search, such a string of unqualified terms will be searched as a phrase. In Raging Search, the same query will result in an AND.

Documents that match your query are assigned a score for ranking purposes based on factors such as the following:

- Where in the page the search terms occur (the title is most important, followed by the first few lines of text)
- The search terms' frequency of occurrence
- The user entering a + in front of the query terms
- The page's popularity, in terms of having lots of pages linked to it, particularly if the links have content related to the page being ranked, and if the links come from a large number of distinct domains
- Proximity of your search terms in the page (how close they are to each other)
- How many of your search terms are present in the document
- Level of the directory in which the page is located (pages in top-level directories get a higher value than those found several levels down)
- Whether your query words and phrases are found early in the page
- Occurrence of words in a metatag (if the words are also used early in the text of the page itself)
- Occurrence of words in hyperlinked ("clickable") text
- Rarity of the query term (pages with the rarer of your query terms will get a higher score than pages that contain a very common query term)

Stop words—AltaVista indexes all words. However, because of the retrieval algorithm, common words may be ignored in your search unless they're within quotation marks.

For sites constructed using "frames," AltaVista indexes the outside of the frame as a page and each individual frame as if it were a separate page.

Unfortunately, the retrieval program sometimes misses records that match your query, usually a result of AltaVista's computers "timing-out" when subjected to a heavy workload. This has resulted in the same query returning, for example, from one to 41 results depending on the time of day and the search mode used. This is most likely to happen when one of your search terms involves more than 100,000 records. If you're doing a combination of terms, and either term is likely to involve such large numbers, be aware that this may happen. Try the same search in another mode (Search Home behaves the worst here). Also, changing the order of your terms can have a significant effect.

AltaVista's Power Search

Power Search (reachable by a link on the Search Tools page) combines most of the searching power of AltaVista's Home and Advanced Search but in menu format. Unfortunately, AltaVista has demoted it to a minor position, then to a hard-to-find link. If AltaVista is not currently hiding it, the following overview should be useful.

Through the use of pull-down windows, radio buttons, and text boxes you can specify:

- **Simple Boolean** (using the "Any of the words" or "All of the words" options in the "Search for" window)
- **Full Boolean** (after selecting "Boolean" in the "Search for" window)
- **Title** search
- **Date**
- **Language**
- **Region**
- **Domain**
- **URL**
- **One result per Web site**
- 10, 20, 30, 40, or 50 **results per page**

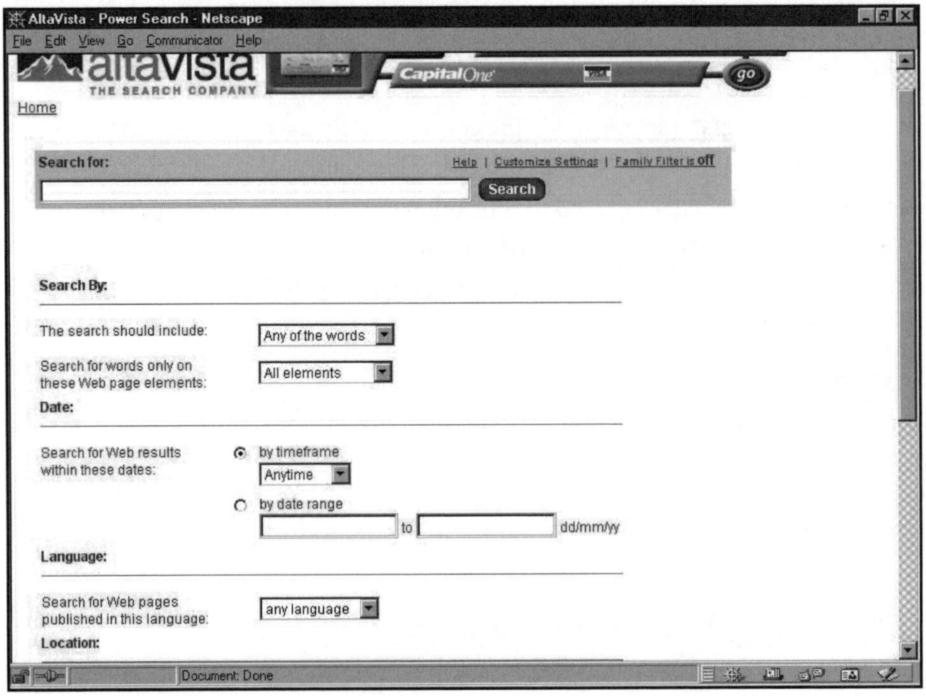

Figure 3.2 AltaVista's Power Search page

Unfortunately, when you use full Boolean in Power Search, relevance ranking is over-ridden. You may therefore want to use Advanced Search for full Boolean queries, particularly when the number of expected records is large.

ALTAVISTA'S ADVANCED SEARCH

AltaVista's "Advanced Search" provides virtually all of the search options of the Search Home mode, plus greater functionality in terms of full Boolean logic and date searching. Unlike Power Search, however, and like the home page, in order to use most of the features you need to know the syntax. The full range of options is not clearly laid out on the page. Full Boolean (but *not* simple Boolean) can be used in Advanced Search and Advanced Search also allows a choice of one result per Web site.

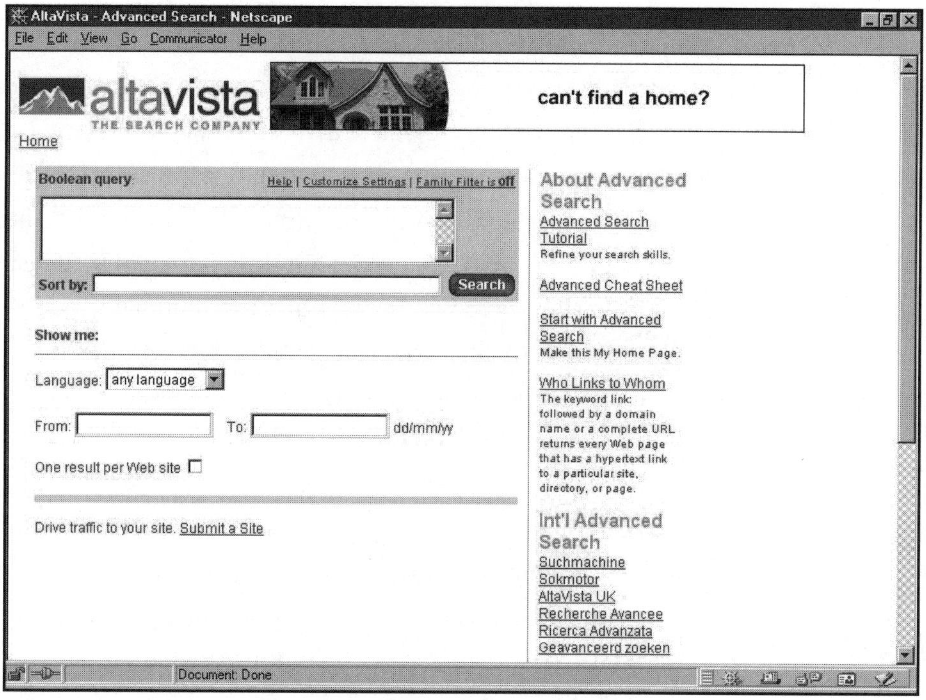

Figure 3.3 AltaVista's Advanced Search page

In Advanced Search, relevance ranking will not take effect unless you also enter terms in the **"Sort by"** box. If you want to have your terms ranked, be sure to put the desired ranking terms there. Your best bet is to choose the most important terms from your Boolean query and place them in the "Sort by" box. If you choose a sort term that was not in your original query, it usually causes your original search to be ANDed with your "Sort by" term. Other records will disappear. The availability of the "Sort by" box for use with full Boolean is about the only advantage Advanced Search has over the other modes. If you need to use full Boolean and you expect a large number of results, that's when you're most likely to need Advanced Search.

AltaVista's Raging Search

Raging Search occupies a precarious position among the AltaVista interfaces. Initially created as a stand-alone service (at ragingsearch.com), it was then moved to some prominence on the Home page, then relegated to a minor, almost-hidden link on the Home page, then to a link on the Search Tools page (but it has remained accessible at its old address). Look for continued vacillation. Raging Search is, on the surface, an extremely simplified interface, with just a basic query box (á la Google). However—and this is its big advantage—it is extremely customizable, and you can put virtually any of AltaVista's search features on your own personalized version of Raging Search. At present, no other search engine provides search customization to this degree.

With the uncustomized page, you can still use many of the most important of AltaVista's regular search features (including prefixes such as title:, url:, link:, etc.). With this interface, for Boolean you are limited to simple Boolean.

Raging Search's real importance shows up in its customization options. The **"Customize"** link allows you to customize the following:

Advanced Search—Your choices here are:

- Query interface (Simple, Advanced, or Power)
- Display of field search boxes (title, URL, host, domain, link, anchor, image)
- Display of the Date Search box
- Family (adult-content) filter
- Site compression (one result per site)
- Ability to open results in a new, or in the same, window

Language—Choose the language you'd like to search in (from a list of 25) and also from one of nine character sets. You can also, on the language-options page, choose to have (or not have) the Translate option appear in results.

Page Layout—You can specify 10, 20, 50, or 100 results per page, the position of the search box on the results page, whether or not you want spelling tips displayed, and whether and where you'd like related searches to appear.

Results Pages—You can add or remove every element of the results record, except the title.

Design—Choose a page-color scheme to match your room, including, fortunately, Guacamole and Pumpkin. You can also choose one of three fonts (Arial/Helvetica, Verdana, Times).

Raging Search provides a lot of easy-to-use power in a clear, uncluttered fashion, but the simplicity also has a cost. In contrast to Power Search, on Raging Search's fully loaded customized page there is no language box or choice of "one result per Web site," nor is there an immediate choice of number of results per page. (You can set these as defaults through the customization pages.) You also lose direct access to AltaVista's many additional features, such as image searching. You also will be missing the integration of some useful resources on results pages, such as RealNames links, etc.

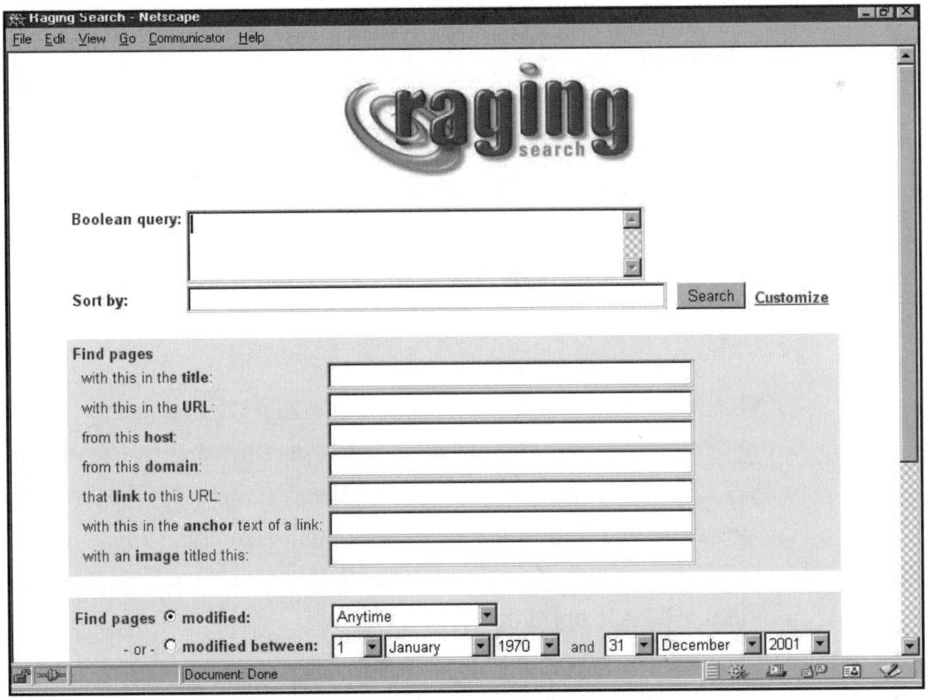

Figure 3.4 Customized version of AltaVista's Raging Search

SEARCH FEATURES

Boolean Logic

Depending on which AltaVista search mode you're using, you can make use of one of the following approaches to Boolean:

Simple Boolean using plus and minus

+term   Put a plus sign immediately in front of the term to insist that a term be present (*+term* acts as an AND).

-term   Put a minus sign immediately in front of the term to exclude records with that term (*-term* acts as a NOT).

Example: +elephants +diet -circus

Simple Boolean by use of pull-down windows

"Any of the words" = OR
"All of the words" = AND

NOT may be indicated by a separate "exclude" box.

Full Boolean

AND

OR

AND NOT—Be sure to use AND NOT, instead of NOT.

( )

Example: diet* AND "weight loss" AND NOT grapefruit*

Note: Lowercase is acceptable.

 NEAR—Though technically not a "Boolean" operator, this "proximity" connector can also be used, and specifies that the words be within 10 words of each other. This is a very powerful way of improving precision and allows greater latitude than searching for words as a phrase. At present, AltaVista is the only major search engine that provides a NEAR option.

Examples: waste NEAR recycling
waste NEAR recycling AND quebec AND directory

> metal AND toxic AND (waste OR scrap) NEAR recycling

If the above operators are used within quotation marks, they'll be treated literally, rather than as operators:

> *Example:* twyford AND "bed and breakfast*"

> (In this example, the asterisk is used to show the use of truncation as well.)

These Boolean variations are available in the different search modes as follows:

Home:

- Uses simple Boolean (+term, -term).
- The default, if terms alone are entered with no qualification, is usually the AND operation.

Power Search:

- For simple Boolean, use the pull-down window choices in the "Search By" window. (Plus and minus don't work in Power Search.)
- The default, if terms alone are entered with no qualification, is the AND operation.
- You can also use full Boolean, but be sure to also choose "Boolean" in the "Search by" window. Relevance ranking is not in effect when you use full Boolean in Power Search.

Advanced Search:

- Uses only full Boolean.
- If you enter two or more terms with no qualifiers, they'll be searched as a phrase.
- Be sure to put terms also in the "Sort by" box if you want your results ranked by relevance.

Raging Search:

- The uncustomized version uses the same approach as Search Home.
- Through use of the customization page, you can choose any of the three Boolean variations.

Field Searching

AltaVista currently has one of the longest lists of searchable fields, though the usefulness of some is minimal (except perhaps to Web page designers). Most fields in AltaVista can be searched by using a prefix in front of the search term, and these prefixes can be used on any of the four AltaVista search modes. Making it easier, most fields are also searchable by use of pull-down windows, or radio buttons and text boxes, depending on the mode.

The following prefixes work in all four search modes:

Title	title:"Boston Globe"	Searches for words or phrases in a page title
URL	url:sec.gov	Searches any contiguous portions of a URL
Host	host:compaq.com	Searches for pages from the specified host
Domain	domain:fr	Searches for the specific domain (country domains such as .fr for France and institutional domains such as .com, .edu, etc.)
Anchor	anchor:"click here"	Searches terms within links (anchors)
Text	text:colchester	Finds pages that contain the specified word "in any part of the visible text of a page" (i.e., the word is not in a link, image, or the URL)
Applet	applet:NervousText	Searches for specific applets
Object	object:Marquee	Searches for (programming) "objects"
Link	link:thomas.gov	Finds pages that link to the specified page
Like	like:www.onstrat.com	Finds pages similar to the specified page
Image	image:beetle.jpg	Searches the term in the file names of images (extension optional). In most cases a better

Image	image:beetle.jpg	way to search for images is to
(cont.)		use the Images Search dis-
		cussed below.

These prefixes can be used in combination. In AltaVista's Search Home, for example, to find pages at Johns Hopkins University's site that are primarily about cancer research there, and that at least mention "prostate," one option would be to use the following query:

+prostate +title:cancer +url:jhu.edu

Date

Date is searchable in Power, Advanced, and Raging Search modes. In all three of those you can search for a specific range of dates. In Power Search and Raging Search there's also a time-frame option ("last 2 weeks," "last month," etc.).

Language

Home, Power, and Advanced modes allow you to search any of 25 languages by using the language pull-down window. The default is "any languages." The languages supported are English, Chinese, Czech, Danish, Dutch, Estonian, Finnish, French, German, Greek, Hebrew, Hungarian, Icelandic, Italian, Japanese, Korean, Latvian, Lithuanian, Norwegian, Polish, Portuguese, Romanian, Russian, Spanish, and Swedish.

Raging Search allows you to specify language (and character set encoding) on its Customize page. (See also the discussion that follows, under "Case-Sensitivity and Diacritics.")

Phrase Searching

" "   Use double quotation marks to search on a phrase in any of the search modes.

Example: "Great Britain"

Any punctuation has the same effect as the use of the quotation marks—e.g., the following three are equivalent:

"frontal lobotomy"
frontal-lobotomy
frontal;lobotomy

The significance of this for searchers is that if you're searching a hyphenated phrase, include the hyphen and it will automatically be treated as a phrase.

AltaVista automatically recognizes millions of commonly used phrases. When two or more words are entered that match a phrase in this list, the string is automatically searched as a phrase. In Advanced mode, any string of words without qualifiers is searched as a phrase. To be safe, if you want to search a phrase, go ahead and use the quotation marks anyway in case your phrase isn't on AltaVista's phrase list.

Truncation

*   Use an asterisk to truncate a search term in any of the search modes.

Example: Mexic*

At least three preceding letters are required. The asterisk will match from 0–5 additional lowercase letters—not capital letters or digits (a search for engin* will not retrieve "engineering"). The asterisk can be used internally (e.g., lab*r will retrieve both labor and labour).

Case-Sensitivity and Diacritics

Searching in all lowercase will retrieve both uppercase and lowercase. For example, "aids" will retrieve aids, AIDS, Aids, aiDs, etc.

If you use capital letters in a search it will force an exact case match for the entire word. For example, "eTRUST" will retrieve "eTRUST" but not "eTrust."

As well as being case-sensitive, AltaVista is also sensitive to accent marks and other diacritical marks, allowing you to distinguish if necessary. This would enable you, for example, to search for resumé rather than resume. If you want to search on diacritics, the problem will be finding them on your keyboard or finding the keyboard codes that represent them. A work-around in any search engine that searches diacritics is to find the appropriate character in a document, then "copy and paste" it into the query. If you're using accent marks frequently, check AltaVista's Help screens and "Language Settings" options (under the "Customize" link in any of the search modes). These give an extensive description of the options that you have. Also, be sure to check out AltaVista's "World Keyboard," found through the Translate link on AltaVista's home, Power, and Advanced pages. The World Keyboard allows you to type using a variety of character sets (and then copy and paste into other applications).

Keep two factors in mind when dealing with diacritics (in AltaVista and elsewhere). First, the content of most Web pages is in English, and words will probably not have been input using diacritics. Most resumés on the Web will not have used the é, but just a plain e, and the plain e will retrieve both. Second, in the case of something like resumé, you will usually have other qualifications in your search, such as a person's name, type of job, etc., which will automatically eliminate most of the irrelevant occurrences of resume. The diacritics of course can become very important when you're searching for non-English sites.

RESULTS PAGES

Output is somewhat different for the four Web search versions. The content of records is virtually the same, but the additional features included on results pages differ considerably. Look for these features to change frequently since AltaVista is continually trying out new options. AltaVista has done an excellent job of integrating a rich variety of resources relevant to the current search into results pages. Look closely at all parts of results pages to take advantage of the range of resources that you may find there. For the records themselves, all of the search modes provide a "Customize" link that allows you to specify exactly which elements you wish to see in a record. All parts except the title are fair game.

Sample Record:

1. United Nations Home Page

This is the official Web Site of the United Nations Headquarters in New York. Here you will find daily UN News, UN Documents and Publications, UN...URL: www.un.org/ Last modified on: 21-Apr-2000 - 6K bytes - in English

Translate More pages from this site ▨ Related pages **Facts about: United Nations Po...**

The brief "abstract" shown comes from the Description metatag. (If the page has no Description metatag, AltaVista will use the first few words from the text of the page itself.) "Translate" will translate the page between English and six other languages. The translate link will only show for those items in one of those seven languages. The "Related pages" link will find pages similar to this page (the same results as when you use the "like:" prefix in a search).

"Facts about" links are present in those records that AltaVista has been able to associate with a particular company, organization, etc. and will display a variety of background information about the company, etc. (Unfortunately, as of this writing the "Facts about..."option seems to be limited almost entirely to U.S. sites, but this could quickly change.) Take advantage of these links. They can lead to a page that includes the following for an organization:

> Link to the home page
> List of registered Web sites
> Map
> Subsidiaries
> Hoovers Capsule
> RealNames link
> Etc.

This data comes from a variety of sources, such as Hoovers, InfoUSA, NavTech, MyWay Corp., and ZIP2.

"More pages from this site" will be present only when only one page per site is shown (what AltaVista refers to as "site compression"). This happens automatically when using Search Home, in Advanced

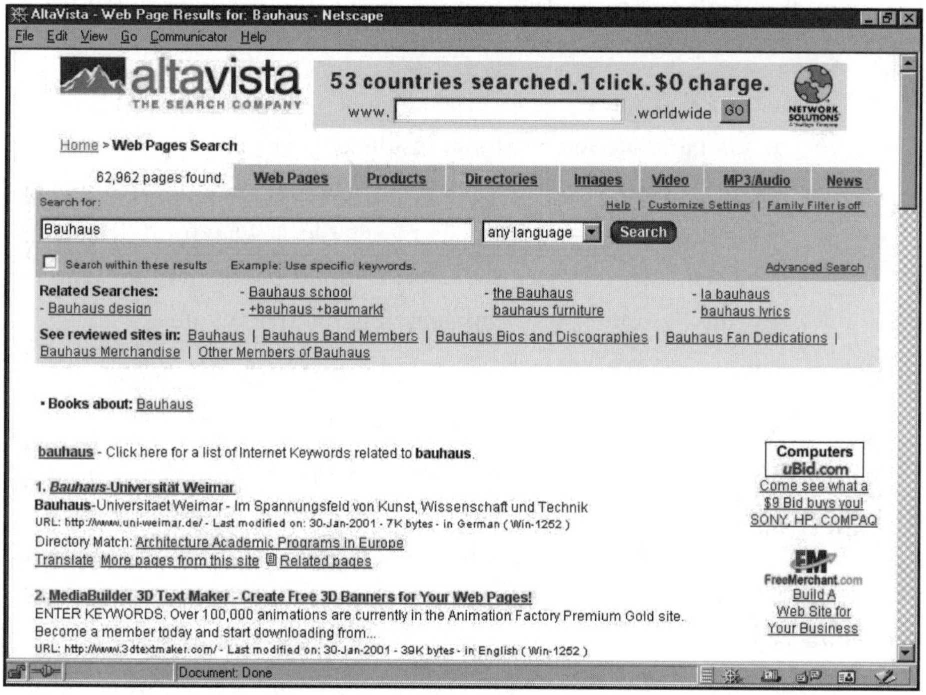

Figure 3.5 AltaVista's results page (Search Home mode)

and Power modes when the "one result per Website" option box has been checked, and in Raging Search when that choice was made on the Customize page. Clicking on the "More pages from this site" link will display the other matching pages from that site. The site compression can be useful if you find results overwhelmed by too many pages from a single site. This is automatically turned off for url: and host: searches. For large hosting sites such as Geocities, the "one page per site" applies at the directory level of the Geocities (or similar) site in order to be able to pick up personal home pages.

AltaVista will provide a maximum of 200 records. So if you're doing one of those fairly rare but sometimes critical searches where you realize you may need to browse more than 200 records, AltaVista won't meet your needs.

The following additional resources may be found on results pages:

Related Searches

(Available on Search Home results pages)

This is a list of up to a dozen or so other searches that contain your search word or phrase. For example, a search on "Bauhaus" suggested such phrases as Bauhaus furniture, Bauhaus design, and Bauhaus Dessau. These can sometimes provide valuable ideas for refining a search.

Tabs for Alternate Searches (Products, News, Images, MP3/Audio, Video, Directories)

(Available on Search Home and Power Search results pages)

Clicking on these tabs will cause your search to be executed in the corresponding AltaVista database. The results will be the same as if you chose those links (Images, etc.) from the Home page and did your search there. By using these tabs on the results pages, the automatic transfer of your search into those databases can save one or more steps. Clicking the Directories tab will execute your search in AltaVista's version of LookSmart.

Internet Keywords

(Available on Search Home and Power Search results pages)

Just before the listing of the first 10 Web sites, you'll sometimes see a link referring to "Internet Keywords." This means that AltaVista has found one of your terms in the RealNames database (of company names, product names, slogans, etc.). Clicking on this link will usually take you directly to the home page for the company, product, etc. This is often a quick and easy way of finding a company home page. If matches are found for more than one of your query words, only one link will be shown (the choice of which one is apparently not "objective"). Queries containing both "BMW" and "Mercedes" showed the link to Mercedes regardless of which company was listed first. Hmm?

Sponsored Listings

These are "paid listings." Commercial sites pay AltaVista to list their sites when specific terms are searched. AltaVista provides some controls to assure that the products and services offered by these sites do relate to the search terms. Note that AltaVista, commendably, clearly separates this list from the regular Web results list.

"Extend Your Search for..."

These links connect you with a variety of AltaVista partners, such as eBay, WorldPages (yellow pages), and the LookSmart Web directory.

Clicking on some of these will cause your request to be carried over directly to the partner site (e.g., in LookSmart.com), while in other cases you'll be taken to the site but will need to re-enter your query. Where the search is carried over, any syntax, such as plus signs and quotation marks, will usually be ignored.

AltaVista's Web Directory

AltaVista is very fickle with regard to its directory partnerships. In a period of less than 2 years, it went from LookSmart to Open Directory, then to a combination of the two, and then back to LookSmart. The directory is directly accessible from the bottom of the AltaVista Search Home page. It's also integrated into search results pages, under "See reviewed sites in...." There you'll find LookSmart categories that match any of your search terms. Individual Web sites from the directory are not incorporated into results listings, as they are in some search engines.

Other Searchable Databases

In addition to the large database of Web sites, AltaVista also provides several other searchable databases that are accessible from its Home page and also reachable by using the tabs on results pages. For very extensive details on searching these databases, check out

AltaVista's help screens, which are very clear, informative, and well-organized.

These collections are very searchable. The same search features that are used in Search Home can be used in most of these collections, including: +term, -term, truncation, quotation marks for phrases, and case-sensitivity. If multiple terms are entered with no qualification, the terms will be ORed. Prefixes such as title: and url: can also be used to some degree, but keep in mind that many of the prefixes used in Search Home are not relevant to some of these collections. For example, because of the nature of the sources, "url:" doesn't really function when searching News.

Images, MP3/Audio, Video, News, and Products

These databases are accessible either by clicking the "Media/Topic Search" link on the Home page, or by clicking the tabs on results pages. Image Search also has a link of its own on the Home page. When the "Media/Topic Search" link is clicked, the resulting page provides a search box followed by radio buttons that allow you to select Products, Directories (LookSmart), Images, Video, MP3/Audio, or News.

On Results pages, when the tabs (Products, Images, etc.) are clicked, the search that was just done is carried into the corresponding database.

Images—At present, AltaVista has one of the best image-searching facilities on the Web. Click on the "Image Search" link, enter a term or two, and click "Search" (see Figure 3.6). Within seconds you have thumbnail versions of matching images. Clicking on the image will take you to the page containing that image.

The images in the collection come from the Web sites indexed by AltaVista in its main index and from "partner sites." The image's file name, nearby text, and page title have all been indexed.

Along with the query box there are two sets of choices you can make to refine your image search:

You can have AltaVista "Show Me" a choice of:

- Photos
- Graphics
- Buttons/Banners
- Color
- Black and White

You can also specify which image collection ("partner site") you wish to search: Web, CDNOW, the Corbis collection, etc.

You can use AltaVista's Home features here, such as +term, -term, truncation, quotation marks for phrases, and case-sensitivity. Among the searchable prefixes that might be of use, consider url:, host:, or domain: in order to get pictures from a particular site or country.

Example: +aptiva +host:ibm.com

If you want to re-use these or an image found on the Web, keep in mind that this material is protected by copyright.

MP3/Audio—Whether you want a sound clip of Churchill's "finest hour" speech or a bit of The Clash you'll be able to find it here.

If you want to choose the file format, with the "Show Me" options you can select MP3, WAV Windows Media, Real, or Other. Under "Sources," you have the options of the Web, FTP, and/or specific Partner Sites, which include CDNOW, Emusic, Epitonic, ARTISTdirect, On24, and Riffage. Most Search Home features (+term, -term, truncation, quotation marks, etc.) can also be used here.

Video—With the rapidly increasing number of sites that provide video and the expanding archive of these online, plus the increased downloading speed used by more and more users, video searching is going to quickly become more and more popular. AltaVista's video search provides an excellent collection for this. The "Show Me" option allows a choice of formats (AVI, MPEG, Quicktime, Windows Media, Real, or Other), and the Sources window gives a choice of video providers, including ABCNews.com, Launch.com, MSNBC, Merrill Lynch, On24, and VIDNET.

The same search features available in Search Home (+term, -term, truncation, quotation marks, etc.) can be used here. For a lot of the video sources, the entire transcript is indexed, meaning you may want to use a lot of the +terms (pluses) to get exactly what you want.

News—This collection includes 19 sources, including newswires (Reuters, PR Newswire, Associated Press, BizWire, and others) and a few leading U.S. newspapers (New York Times, Washington Post, Los Angeles Times, and others). The most recent 14 days are covered. Expect a 2 to 3 hour greater delay for news

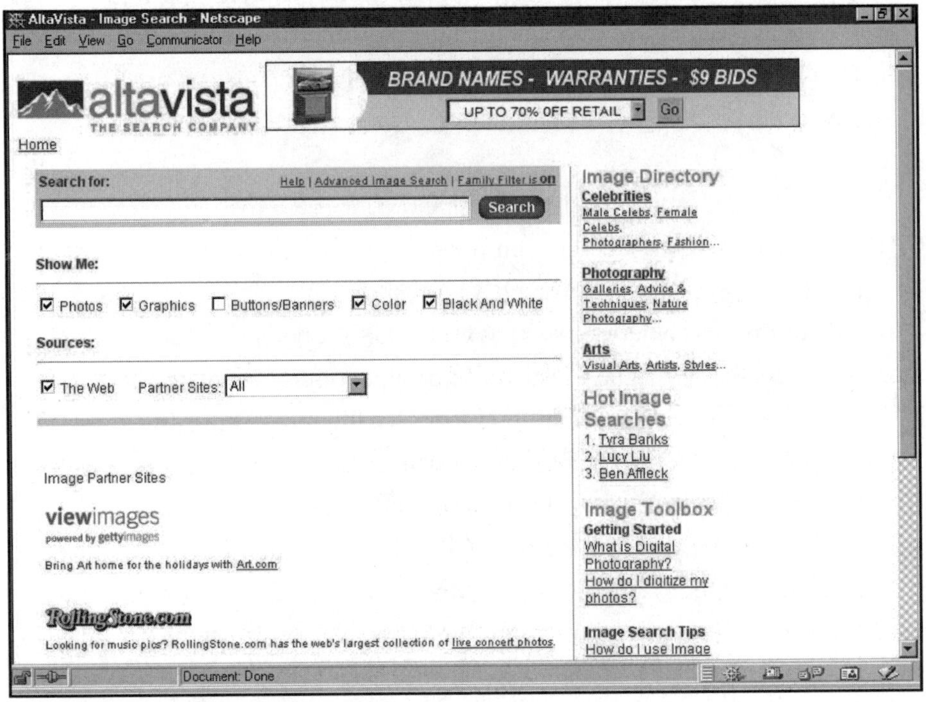

Figure 3.6 AltaVista's Image search

stories than when accessing primary news sites such as the MSNBC, CNN, and BBC sites.

Whether you get to News search from the "More News" link on AltaVista's home page or by clicking on the News tab on results pages, you can use most of the same search features (+term, -term, truncation, quotation marks, etc.) that you use in other Home searches. The News search also offers a date option where you can choose news items from the last 6 hours, 12 hours, 24 hours, 7 days, or 14 days. You can also specify a news category and source.

Products—This is AltaVista's own shopping site, which has lots of places to spend money. You can search using +term, -term, truncation, and phrases (quotation marks).

OTHER PORTAL FEATURES

In 2001, AltaVista greatly decreased its portal offerings in a move back toward a purer "search engine" identity. It removed such things as Clubs, Photo Albums, Home Pages, Message Boards, Chat, and the personalized "My AltaVista." It did retain, though, quite a number of useful "portal-type" tools. Several of these are displayed on the Home page (mainly under "Search Tools"), and more are found by clicking on the "Search Tools" link. (Keep in mind that AltaVista has a seemingly uncontrollable urge to move things around, so you may find the location of these tools changing frequently.)

Shopping—Under Find Products or similar links, you will find a link to AltaVista's shopping site, and—depending upon AltaVista's current partnerships—such things as auctions.

Search Tools—This section lists a selection of frequently used tools and links. By clicking on "Search Tools," you are taken to the "Email, Tools and Search Centers" page, which includes more tools and links to Channels ("Search Centers").

Under "Search Tools" on the Home page, you will find:
- **Links to Image Search and the Translate feature** (discussed elsewhere in this chapter)
- **Email**—AltaVista's free e-mail service
- **Maps and Driving Directions**—Powered by MAPBLAST
- **Yellow Pages**—Powered by WorldPages.com
- **People Finder**—White pages powered by WorldPages.com
- **Etc.**

More Tools—In addition to the tools listed on the Home page, you will find links to Power Search and Raging Search, as well as specialty searches such as Education Search and Government

Search. The latter two options search, respectively, only the .edu and .gov sites in AltaVista's Web index.

Search Centers (Channels)—The Email, Tools & Search Centers page lists about a dozen specialty topic channels, most of which are powered by AltaVista partners such as Cars.com, uBid.com, eFrontCareers.com, ebix.com, Move.com, and Trip.com. Among the channels are the following:

Autos

Auctions

Careers

Entertainment

Insurance

News

Real Estate

Shopping

Travel

Tech

World

The content of these channels varies considerably. Some, such as Insurance, are basically shopping sites, while others, such as Careers, offer a variety of useful, specialized tools. In some cases, the channels also display the relevant categories from AltaVista's version of LookSmart.

OTHER FEATURES

Translate

The Translate feature (powered by SYSTRAN Translation Software) that was discussed earlier as an option appearing in results records is also available as "stand-alone." You'll find the Translate link listed with the services on the AltaVista Search Home page. Clicking on it will lead to a box into which you can enter up to about 30 lines of text and have it translated either way between English and French, German, Italian, Portuguese, Spanish, Japanese, Korean, or Chinese. It will also translate from Russian to English, German to French, and French to German.

The Translate page also provides a convenient World Keyboard option that brings up a small keyboard window that allows you to input text in the translation box in French, German, Italian, Portuguese, or Spanish character sets. Besides using this for translating, the text you enter into the text box using these character sets can also be copied and pasted into other applications such as word processors or e-mail messages.

International Editions

The AltaVista Around the World link at the bottom of most search pages leads to the international versions of AltaVista. There are country-specific versions for Australia, Brazil, Canada, Denmark, France, Germany, India, Ireland, Italy, Netherlands, Portugal, Sweden, and the U.K. In addition, there are partner sites in 11 other countries (Yupi.com, Info Media Systems, Netway, Belgacom, Kaare Danielsen, Blue Window, Sina.com, Alam Malaysia, Apex Systems, e-sekai, and Pacific Access).

Family Filter

This option is located to the right of the query box on the Search Home, Power, and Advanced Search pages. It allows you to set the filter to filter all content or just multimedia (image, video, and audio) content. Password protection (for turning the filter on and off) can also be set up.

SUMMARY OF ALTAVISTA

AltaVista is one of the largest and most powerful of the Web search engines. As in its beginning, AltaVista's emphasis is once again on searching, rather than being a portal. It provides a powerful array of search features plus access to additional databases such as images and audio. It now provides a modest but useful collection of other tools, including phone directories, news searches, and its translation feature. With the addition of the Power Search option, AltaVista not only provides very strong search capabilities, but makes the options clearly accessible.

Use the Home page when you have a very simple search that needs no qualifications applied. Use Advanced Search ONLY when you really need full Boolean. Try Power Search or Raging Search, and see if their particular balances of simplicity, menus, and customization suit your own personal searching style. Except for full Boolean (which you may not need frequently anyway), Power Search provides virtually all of AltaVista's search options in an easy-to-use format.

The serious searcher—no, almost any searcher—should explore the nooks and crannies of AltaVista. For any search where it's important that no relevant items be missed, this is one of the search engines that must be used.

CHAPTER 4

Excite

www.excite.com

OVERVIEW

As a search engine, Excite is in the midrange functionally, but as a portal it's outstanding. In terms of the consumer-researcher spectrum, Excite is definitely positioning itself on the consumer end. In terms of size, its database is in the midrange. For searching, Excite has full Boolean capabilities and phrase searching, but minimal field searching and no case sensitivity or user-controlled truncation. The advanced version allows a little field searching and a choice of format options, but allows less flexibility for Boolean. Excite also provides a "Precision Search" interface page, which is a bare-bones version of the home page, without the portal features.

As a portal, Excite stands out from the pack with its home page's emphasis on news and personalization, allowing any user to tailor it to his or her own needs, especially in terms of headline news (and personalized news alerts). Additional features, including sports

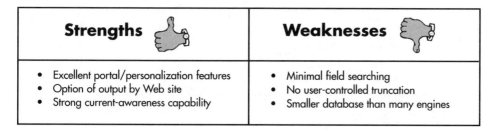

Strengths 👍	Weaknesses 👎
• Excellent portal/personalization features • Option of output by Web site • Strong current-awareness capability	• Minimal field searching • No user-controlled truncation • Smaller database than many engines

scores and TV listings, can also be selected by the user to appear on the personalized home page.

Excite has indexed about 250 million Web pages.

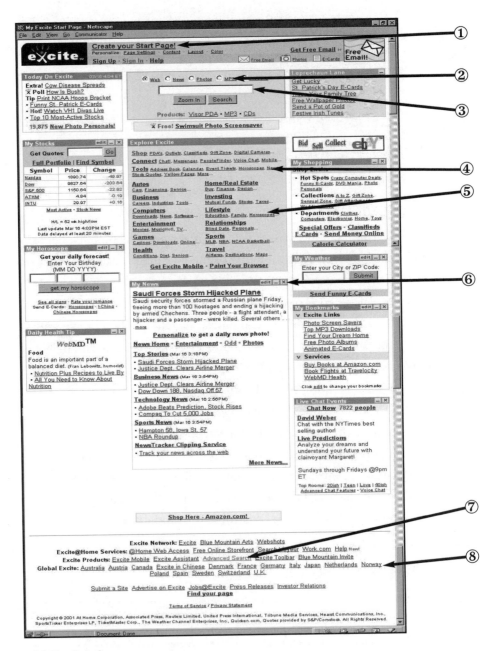

Figure 4.1 Excite's home page

Excite's Home Page

① **Personalizing Options**—Options for selecting content, layout, and colors of the Excite home page. The "Sign in" link enables you to access your own personal page from someone else's computer

② **Other Searchable Databases:**
  • Web
  • News
  • Photos
  • MP3s
  • Products

③ **Query Box**—Words, Boolean operators, etc., can be entered.

④ **Portal Features**—Yellow Pages, White Pages, Classifieds, Stock Quotes, News, Horoscopes, Crosswords, etc.

⑤ **"Channels"**—Excite's channels with directory and added tools

⑥ **News**

⑦ **Link to Advanced Search Option**—This leads to the screen where you can choose format options and number of results per page, and also do a minimal amount of field searching.

⑧ **Links to Excite's International Versions**

What Happens Behind the Scenes

Excite utilizes a combination of ranking based upon popularity (link analysis) and Excite's earlier ranking technology (concept-searching), which involves semantic matching and other factors. Excite does not index some metatags. (This can cause some very relevant records to be missed in a search.) It does index the Description metatag. For records where the Description metatag is present, that is what will be used as the abstract that appears in search results. Otherwise, Excite constructs the abstract from the first few words of the page.

If a string of terms is entered with no qualifiers (such as Boolean operators), Excite will, in effect, "OR" all of the words and also retrieve records with related words it has identified. Retrieved records are sorted by relevance.

EXCITE'S ADVANCED SEARCH

When the "Advanced Search" link (at the bottom of Excite's home page) is clicked, you see the screen represented in Figure 4.2.

Excite's Advanced Search provides the following options:

① The ability to search:
- **The Web**
- Selected Web Sites **(Excite's directory)**

② The ability to use **Boolean** on **words or phrases**, but by using pull-down window choices, instead of the operators themselves

③ The option of displaying 10, 20, 30, or 50 **records per page**
The option of **displaying**:
- Titles only
- Titles and summaries

④ Choice of searching in 11 **languages**

⑤ Ability to specify **country** of **origin/domain type** (.com, .edu, etc.)

SEARCH FEATURES

Boolean Logic

Boolean Logic in Excite's Home Page Version

Simple Boolean—In conjunction with the default "concept" search, you can use the following options, but only with the home page version—not in Advanced Search mode:

+term—Put a plus sign immediately in front of the term to insist that a term be present.

-term—Put a minus sign immediately in front of the term to exclude records with that term.

Example: +java -coffee

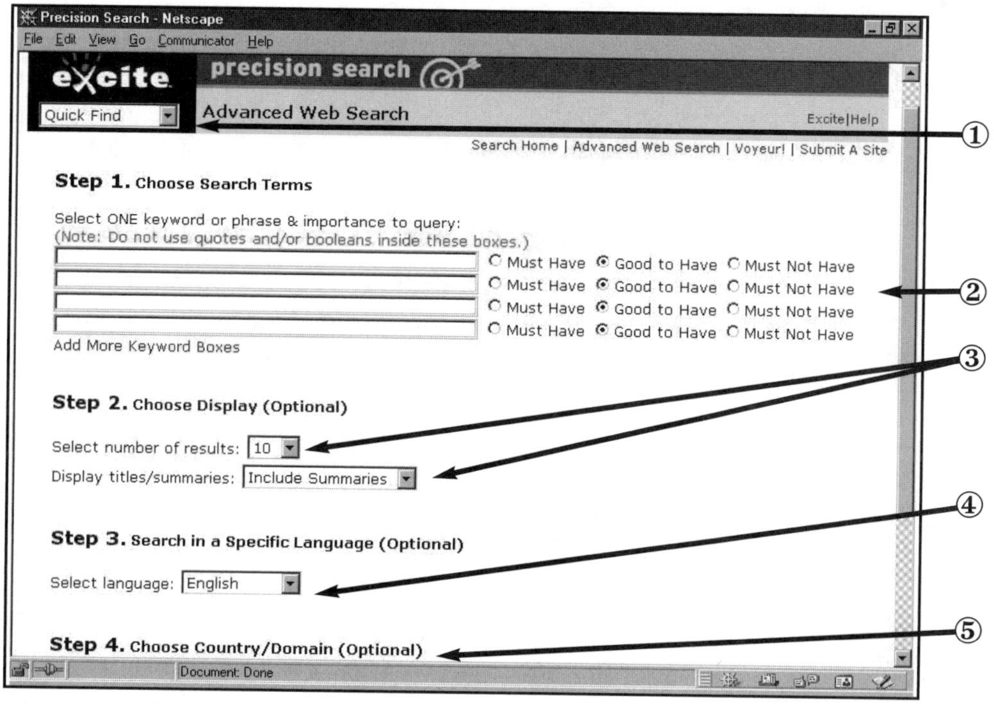

Figure 4.2 Excite's Advanced Search page

Full Boolean—On the Excite home page (again, not in Advanced Search) you can use the following Boolean operators. When you do, concept-based retrieval is turned off. When using these operators, Excite requires that these operators be capitalized.

AND

OR

NOT

( )

Example: "real estate" AND Chestertown

NOT commercial

Boolean Logic in Excite's Advanced Version

In the Advanced version, the only Boolean possible is with the use of the radio buttons. For each set of terms you enter in the query boxes, you can choose:

Good to Have (equals an "OR")

Must Have (equals an "AND")
Must Not Have (equals a "NOT")

Note that this approach (windows) does **not** allow searching of an expression with multiple terms for more than one of the concepts, such as:

(Mexico OR Mexican) AND (pots OR pottery)

For questions such as this, go back to the main Excite page and just try "Mexican pottery" and let Excite do its automatic concept searching. If that doesn't work, try the full Boolean statement on Excite's home page.

Field Searching

Excite's field searching is very limited, providing only specifically searchable fields: language, country, and domain type.

Language—In Advanced Search, use the pull-down language window to search only pages in the following eleven languages: English, Chinese, Dutch, French, German, Italian, Japanese, Norwegian, Portuguese, Spanish, and Swedish.

Country—In Advanced Search, use the pull-down "Country/Domain" window to search only pages from one of 29 countries/continents. The defaults is "All Countries."

Domain Type—In Advanced Search, use the same window as for country to search only pages from .com, .edu, .net, .org, .gov, or .mil domains. You cannot specify both country and domain type in the same search, except for the U.S.

Phrase Searching

" "   Use double quotation marks (use of this does not turn off concept-based retrieval)

Example: "King Albert"

Truncation

Truncation is not available per se, but the effect is achieved (somewhat) in the concept-based searching done automatically by the Excite program. Remember that when you use the Boolean AND, OR, or NOT, the concept-based retrieval is turned off. Therefore, if you're going to use the full Boolean as a substitute for truncation the safe thing to do is to specifically enter the variant endings.

Example: home AND (brew OR brewing OR brewed) AND (ingredient OR ingredients)

This particular example is another case where leaving it to the Excite program's automatic truncation works best. Just entering "home brewing ingredients" (without the quotation marks) works considerably better here than relying on the fancier Boolean statement.

Case-Sensitivity

Excite is not case-sensitive and cannot distinguish between uppercase and lowercase.

RESULTS PAGES

Though search options are pretty limited in Excite, the results pages can provide a variety of information resources besides just the Web pages from Excite's main index.

When searching from Excite's main page, in addition to the Web results you'll find (depending on the particular search) the following:

Links to the following specialized searches:

- **Directory Search** (search of the LookSmart directory)
- **News Search**
- **Photo Search**
- **Audio/Video Search**

For cities, countries, U.S. sports teams, etc., a "Quick Results" box with links to a variety of resources related to the topics, such as:

- For countries and cities—maps and travel guides

- For companies—stock quotes, company profiles and financials, etc.
- For entertainers—biographies, discographies, etc.
- For U.S. colleges and universities—map, profile, phone numbers, etc.
- For movies—stars, directory reviews, show locations and times (localized for your user profile), etc.

Web Results

Format Options—Choice of output formats can be made in the home page mode only after a results page has been displayed. In Advanced Mode, formats can be selected from a pull-down window. In either mode, the format options are:

- **Full Description**
- **Show Titles Only**
- **View by URL**

The "View by URL" option is useful when encountering a large number of pages from the same site. Arranging retrieved pages by site makes it easier for a searcher to determine the source of the information, and thus its potential relevance. However, when you choose this option, only the top 30 sites are shown.

In Advanced Search, you are also given the option of displaying 10, 20, 30, 40, or 50 results per page.

Summaries:

> Chemical Online: Virtual community for the chemical process industry
> **URL:** http://www.chemicalonline.com
> Daily news and product updates for professionals in the chemical industry-
> Information on manufacturing,

Titles only:

> Chemical Online: Virtual community for the chemical process industry
> **URL:** http://www.chemicalonline.com

List by Web Site (will only include approximately the top 30):
> www.neis.com
>> chemical industry—The Chemical Industry Home Page—
>> The Chemical Industry Home Page

> sci.mond.org
> > Society of Chemical Industry
>
> www.ciit.org
> > CIIT WWW Server Home Page

In some searches, Excite will dig into other resources for you and return some very useful information. For example, if you do a search on a medical term, such as laparoscopy, you'll find the definition (from Health Illustrated Encyclopedia on adam.com) on your results page.

EXCITE'S DIRECTORY

Excite's directory can be accessed primarily in three ways: (1) The categories listed on Excite's home page under "Explore Excite" lead to channels. In each of those channels, in addition to other tools, you'll find the relevant directory categories, which can then be browsed. (2) The Web Directory link on results pages allow searching of the directory. The same search operators as used on Excite's home page (+, -, AND, " ", etc.) can be used. (3) A search of the directory is done automatically when you do any search. Hits from the directory, both categories and Web sites, are incorporated into search results lists. These are identifiable by the presence in the record of "Excite Category Match." Clicking the category shown there will take you to that category in the directory.

OTHER SEARCHABLE DATABASES

In addition to the Web database, on Excite's home page four other searchable databases are provided—**Photos, News, Products,** and **MP3/Audio Search.**

Photos

This option provides access to over 750,000 Web users' photos from Excite's Webshots.com and over 20,000 news photos from Reuters and Associated Press (AP).

Figure 4.3 Excite's results page

News

Excite's News Search covers Web news, news wires, and news photos. "Web news" covers over 300 online publications. The news wires portion consists of over a dozen news wire services from around the world. News photos come from AP and Reuters.

On results pages, Excite will display 10 records, showing the title, date, and source. News articles go back approximately 5 days. Links at the tops of results pages allow you to view results by headlines, publication, or date. Records also contain a "Related Articles" link that will lead you to similar articles on the topic

For a fuller treatment of news, be sure to look at the News section on Excite's home page—it provides even more news options, including NewsTracker, Excite's free alerting service.

MP3/Audio

Excite's Audio/Video Search includes sound and video clips with music, excerpts from radio and TV broadcasts, speeches, etc.

In the query box you can use quotation marks for phrases and pluses and minuses to limit your search.

At the top of the results pages is an option to show "All," "MP3," or "Other Audio."

PORTAL AND PERSONALIZATION FEATURES

Channels ("Explore Excite")

The greatest strength of the channels is the wide variety of additional tools presented within the channels. The 12 channels, found just beneath the query box on Excite's main page, are:

- Autos
- Business
- Computers
- Entertainment
- Games
- Health

- Home/Real Estate
- Investing
- Lifestyle
- Relationships
- Sports
- Travel

Browse through at least two or three channels that most interest you. You'll find a variety of useful tools, special directories, buyers' guides, message boards, channel-specific news, etc. An example of a channel page (Education) is shown in Figure 4.4. A compilation of many of the special tools will be found under the little "More" link on the home page.

Personalization Options

Excite's approach is centered around an information service that allows the user to extensively personalize what's seen on the Excite home page. Searching is but one aspect that the user can choose. While Excite is not usually my first choice for a Web search, I've

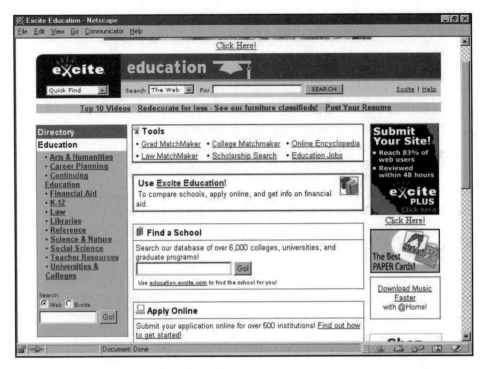

Figure 4.4 Excite Channel—Education

selected its home page as the default page for my browser. By going directly to my personalized Excite page when I log on, I can see news headlines on topics of interest to me, check the shape of my meager stock portfolio, and—most importantly—get the latest news relevant to any one of several personally tailored current awareness searches (currently included, as you might suspect, is one on "search engines").

Most of the sections of the Excite home page are personalizable in terms of specific content and location on the page. A brief description of the more significant of these personalizable sections follows.

Personalize Options

This section, found at the top of the home page, has a link for making Excite your start page. There you can choose layout and color combinations (including Grape Popsicle and Saltwater Taffy) and very detailed calendar and address book pages.

My News

In the "My News" section, by clicking on the "Edit" button you can elect to have headlines displayed from the following broad topics, or from numerous subcategories within those topics. You can also specify the order in which they're listed.

• Top Stories	• Business
• Sports	• Technology
• Politics	• International
• Odd	• Industries
• Entertainment	• Health
• Science	• Stocks

My Stocks

Excite's "Stocks" section allows you to track market indices, or to create your own detailed portfolio of holdings and then view them in any one of several formats.

My Reminders

You can choose to be reminded of holidays and other events, or add your own events and specify how far before the event you wish to be reminded. A small notepad can also be included.

My Weather

Using your ZIP Code, Excite will provide your local weather report and weather for other cities of your choice, plus phases of the moon, tides, and times for sunrise and sunset.

My Bookmarks

Just what the name implies.

My Sports Scores

Excite offers a chart of current sports action for the sports and teams you select.

NewsTracker

"NewsTracker" is an optional category in the news section that deserves special attention because of its relevance to searching.

NewsTracker is a free "clipping service" that accesses over 350 sources, including major news wires, magazines, and newspapers. With NewsTracker it's easy to set up to 20 current-awareness searches to enable you to easily keep up with news events relating to topics of interest. In setting up searches, full Boolean is not available, but radio buttons provide simplified Boolean. NewsTracker is a service most serious searchers will want to explore.

My Searches

This section enables you to store *Web* searches (in contrast to the NewsTracker *news* searches), which you can rerun without having to rekey them.

Tools, Connect, and Shop

This is a collection of tools, among which are:

- Address Book
- Airline Tickets
- Calendar
- Classifieds (search and/or place ads)
- Event Tickets (from tickets.com)
- Horoscopes
- Maps/Directions (from MAPBLAST)
- Movie Times
- People Finder
- Site Index
- Stock Quotes (takes you to Excite's Investing channel, run by Quicken)
- Yellow Pages (powered by WorldPages)

Shopping

Of course.

People and Chat

Chat, message boards, clubs, personals, etc.

Other Optional Sections

These include **TV listings** and **movies**, local events, lottery numbers, cartoons, and varied other odds and ends.

OTHER FEATURES

Global Excite

Excite has country-specific versions or language-specific interfaces for the following:

- Australia
- Austria
- Canada
- Denmark
- Excite in Chinese
- France
- Germany
- Italy
- Japan
- Netherlands
- Spain
- Sweden
- Switzerland
- U.K.

Certainly, if you're in these countries, you may want to make use of these versions, but even if you're not, but are doing research on non-U.S. companies, consider these sites. They contain information you may not find on the generic Excite.

"More"

This small and unassuming link (under "Tools") is full of good things. What Excite has done basically is to gather together into a single categorized list the various tools that are scattered through the various channels and subchannels. Take a look.

Voyeur

This link, found near the query box, allows a view of what other people are searching. It's refreshed every 30 minutes.

Excite Toolbar

This is a small, downloadable program that puts a miniature version of Excite on your Internet Explorer (but not Netscape Navigator) browser screen. To download the program, go to the "Excite Toolbar" link found at the bottom of Excite's home page. After downloading, it will appear as a one-line toolbar beneath your other Internet Explorer toolbars, and it contains an Excite query box and pull-down windows for news, stock searches, news, reference, etc. You can choose which search options you would like to have displayed by going to the "edit" option under the Excite logo link on the toolbar.

"PRECISION SEARCH" PAGE

Since the simplicity of Google's search page was shown to have excellent consumer appeal, AltaVista mimicked it with its "Raging Search" interface. So with those companies now providing such interfaces, Excite created its "Precision Search" page, as shown in Figure 4.5. This is accessible directly at www.excite.com/search or wherever you find a link labeled "Precision Search."

Figure 4.5 Excite's Precision Search page

As with AltaVista's Raging Search, Excite's Precision Search page initially put the main focus on the query box, which has the same functionality as the search query box on Excite's home page.

As this book goes to press, the terminology can be seen as a bit confusing. Both the Precision Search Page and the Advanced Search page are labeled "Precision Search." All results pages, whether you got to them through Excite's home page, the Precision Search page, or the Advanced Search page, are labeled "Precision Search." The "Search Home" link found on results pages leads to the "Precision Search" page, not to the Excite home page. All this does make sense, though not necessarily immediate sense. Hopefully by the time you're reading this, it will have been made clearer, in which case forget I said anything.

SUMMARY OF EXCITE

Excite is a good search engine and a very good portal. On the searching side, with its use of link analysis combined with its other ranking factors, it can retrieve useful records without your having to put too much effort into planning the search, especially on very general topics. Whereas for a while, Excite was very nicely integrating a variety of resources directly into its results listings, it has more recently "simplified" (some might say "dumbed-down") its results pages. It also eliminated the helpful suggested search terms and "more like this" feature. If you're doing an exhaustive search, try Excite along with a couple of the larger engines. There is a good chance Excite will retrieve some additional, relevant items.

For the serious searcher, one of Excite's greatest strength lies in its news resources—especially NewsTracker, which provides an excellent free news clipping service. If you have a topic on which you'd like to keep up-to-date, try this out. For those of you who are providing information support to other Web users, consider telling them about Excite's NewsTracker and personalizable home page (but have them add a couple of other search engines in the "My Bookmarks" section of the page). The kind of benefits this provides are comparable to what organizations had to pay many thousands of dollars for just a few years ago.

CHAPTER 5

Fast Search
www.alltheweb.com

OVERVIEW

Fast Search, from Norway's Fast Search and Transfer (FAST), is now one of the largest Web search engines and is indeed very fast. It's simple to use, in part because of the very limited functionality shown on the home page. With the addition of the Advanced Search mode, functionality has been increased tremendously, particularly with regard to field searching. The Fast Search relevance-ranking algorithm may be significantly more effective than that of some other major search engines. The FAST company is in the business of selling its technology to search engine providers, so look for an increasing FAST presence in some other search services. Fast Search contains over 575 million pages.

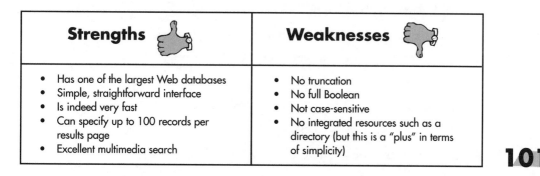

Strengths 👍	Weaknesses 👎
• Has one of the largest Web databases • Simple, straightforward interface • Is indeed very fast • Can specify up to 100 records per results page • Excellent multimedia search	• No truncation • No full Boolean • Not case-sensitive • No integrated resources such as a directory (but this is a "plus" in terms of simplicity)

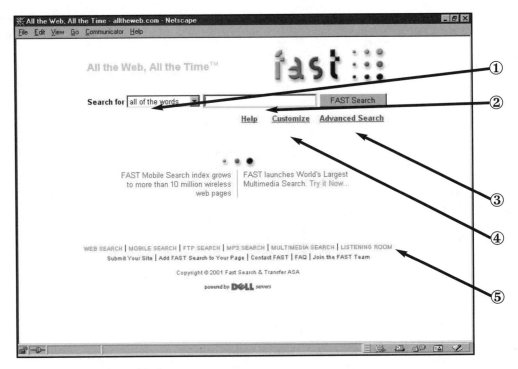

Figure 5.1 Fast Search's home page

FAST SEARCH'S HOME PAGE (SIMPLE SEARCH)

① **Search Options:**

   • All of the words   • Any of the words   • The exact phrase

② **Query Box**—You can enter single words or phrases or use simplified Boolean (+term, -term)

③ **Link to Advanced Search**

④ **Link to Customization options**—Language settings, Offensive Content Reduction, and number of word filter boxes (for Advanced Search)

⑤ **Links to:**

   • **FTP Search** (link to Lycos' FTP Search)

   • **MP3 Search** (link to Lycos' MP3 Search)

- **Multimedia Search**
- **Listening Room** (link to Lycos' Music Search)
- **FA Premier** —"Largest Soccer Site" [Can you guess the favorite sport at Fast Search?]
- **Help** screen and information about the FAST Search company

WHAT HAPPENS BEHIND THE SCENES

The focus of the Fast Search organization is on the search technology. A key objective in the design of Fast Search is to provide a search system that is very scalable in terms of both the number of searches that can be handled and the size of the database. Actually, the company isn't trying to have this site compete with the other services as a popular interface; rather, it's trying to sell its technology to other services. Lycos was the first large Web search service to partner with Fast Search and is now using the Fast Search technology and database. Fast Search uses a "massively parallel architecture" and simultaneously sends each query to a bank of nodes, each holding 5 million documents. Results are then gathered and returned to the user. This does indeed result in a very fast response.

The retrieval program incorporates relevance-ranking algorithms that analyze documents both statically and dynamically—i.e., evaluating the record on its own (e.g., link analysis) and in the context of the specific query. Fast Search indexes all terms (no "stop words") and for queries that contain no qualifiers, it will AND all of the terms that the user enters.

FAST SEARCH'S ADVANCED SEARCH

Whereas the only search feature provided in Simple Search is simplified Boolean, Fast Search's Advanced Search provides that plus extensive, easy field searching. The Advanced page shows the following:

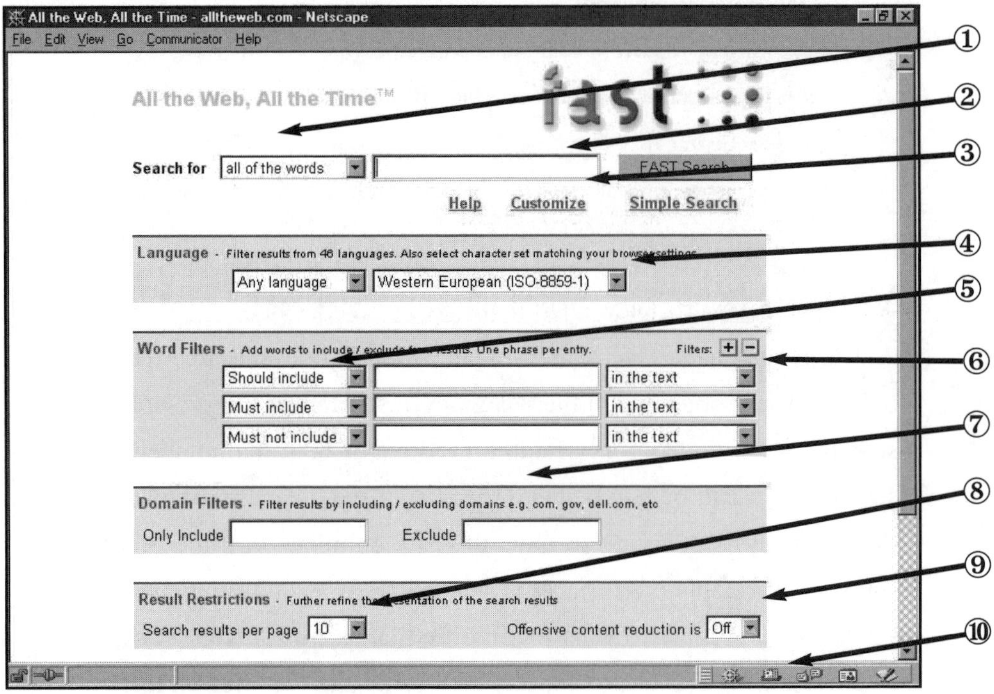

Figure 5.2 Fast Search's Advanced Search page

① **Search Options:** All of the words, Any of the words, The exact phrase

② **Query Box**—You can enter single words or phrases or use simplified Boolean (+term, -term), phrases, or (term1 term2) for an OR.

③ **Customization Link**—For setting language options, offensive-content filter, and number of word-filter boxes

④ **Language window**—Choice of searching only those pages in any of 31 languages

⑤ **Pull-down windows to specify:**

- **Should include** [= OR]
- **Must include** [= AND]
- **Must not include** [= NOT]

⑥ **Field Qualifiers:**

- **Text**
- **Title**
- **Link name**

- **URL**
- **Link to URL**

⑦ **Domain Filters**—To limit to or exclude a specific domain (mit.edu, .fr, .com)

⑧ **Number of Results per page**—10, 25, 50, 75, or 100

⑨ **Offensive Content Reduction**—Can be turned on or off

⑩ **Links to:**

- **FTP Search** (link to Lycos' FTP Search)
- **MP3 Search** (link to Lycos' MP3 Search")
- **Multimedia**
- **Listening Room** (link to Lycos' Music Search)

SEARCH FEATURES

Boolean

In either version of Fast Search, you have only a **"simplified"** Boolean option:

Boolean Logic in Fast Search's Simple Search:

The Boolean AND and OR are presented as a pull-down window option:

"all of the words"

"any of the words"

You can also use (in the query box):

+term   to insist that a term be present

-term   to eliminate any page containing the term

Since the default "all of the words" implies the "AND" you don't have to specify the "+", but doing so will do no harm.

If you want to do a Boolean query that includes alternate terms (synonyms) for one of your concepts, use the "any of the words" option and the following format:

+norway +(agriculture agricultural) +revenues

This would insist that both the word "norway" and the word "revenues" be present, and the records must contain either "agriculture" or "agricultural." The parentheses around a pair of words equates to an

OR in Fast Search. The order of the words in your query doesn't seem to have a significant effect on which records will be retrieved first.

Boolean Logic in Fast Search's Advanced Search

In Advanced Search, Boolean works the same way as in Simple Search. The above options apply, as in the home page version, plus you have:

"Word Filter" boxes that have pull-down windows for

"should include"

"must include"

"must not include"

Note: You can do a search on Fast Search's Home page (Simple Search), then click on the "Advanced Search" link and your query will be automatically transferred to the Advanced Search page.

Field Searching

Fast Search's Advanced Search mode allows searching by Language, Title, Link Name, URL, and Link To URL.

Language

In the Advanced version, Fast Search provides a language panel with a pull-down window for searching in 47 languages which, among others, include the following:

- Bulgarian
- Catalan
- Czech
- Danish
- Dutch
- English
- Estonian
- Finnish
- French
- German
- Greek
- Hebrew
- Hungarian
- Icelandic
- Italian
- Latvian
- Lithuanian
- Norwegian
- Polish
- Portuguese
- Romanian
- Russian
- Slovenian
- Spanish
- Swedish

The fields Title, Link Name, URL, and Link To URL are all searchable by using the pull-down window on the right side of the "Word Filters Panel" and entering the appropriate term in the adjoining query box. In each case, also specify "Should include," "Must include," or "Must not include" in the Boolean window on the left side of the panel.

Title

Choose "Title" from the pull-down window on the right of the "Word Filters" boxes. Either words or phrases can be searched.

Link Name

Use the pull-down window on the right of the "Word Filters" boxes. This field searches for the text that's included in hypertext links—i.e., the underlined, clickable text. For example, if you wish to find pages having a link to the company Telstra, one way to do it will be to use this field with the word "telstra." That would retrieve records with that word linked. The other way will be to use the "Link To URL" discussed below.

URL

To retrieve pages from a specific Web site, use the pull-down window on the right of the "Word Filters" boxes and enter the URL in the text box.

> *Examples:*
>> ox.ac.uk
>> bodley.ox.ac.uk

Also, under the "Domain Filters" section, you can limit or exclude by either the type of domain (.com, .edu, .gov, etc.), or by domain name (e.g., onstrat.com).

Link to URL

Use the pull-down window on the right of the "Word Filters" boxes and enter the URL in the text box.

This will search for pages that link to a particular URL.

Note: All multiple words entered in the "Word Filters" boxes are treated as phrases.

Phrase Searching

" " Phrases can be searched using quotation marks.

Also, though, multiple words are automatically treated as phrases in the "Word Filters" query boxes in Advanced Search.

Truncation

As of this writing, Fast Search provides no truncation capability.

Case-Sensitivity

Fast Search is *not* case-sensitive.

RESULTS PAGES

Fast Search delivers 10 results per page as the default. On the Advanced Search page, you can specify 10, 25, 50, 75, or 100 results per page. The ability to display a large number of records per page is very useful when you may need to do a lot of browsing. For both Simple and Advanced, the search options are shown at the top and/or bottom of results to allow easy modification.

Sample Record:

3 POLYVINYL ACETATE DISPERSION (PVA) (GOST 18992-80)
POLYVINYL ACETATE DISPERSION (PVA) (GOST 18992-80) Homopolymeric polyvinyl acetate dispersion (course-dispersion) is product of emulsion polymerization in water of vinyl acetate in the presence of initiator and protective colloid of polyvinyl alcohol
http://www.azot.lg.ua/products/e_pva.html

DIRECTORY

Fast Search has no directory associated with it.

OTHER SEARCHABLE DATABASES

You can get to the following databases by using the navigation bar at the top of both the Simple Search and Advanced Search pages:

- **FTP Search**—Downloadable files
- **MP3 Search**—Over 1 million MP3 files
- **Multimedia Search**—17 million pictures, videos, and audio files. An excellent, large, and easy-to-use collection. See the discussion of this on page 49.
- **Listening Room**—For listening to clips from new bands

Clicking on any of these, except Multimedia, will take you to the corresponding option in Lycos Advanced Search. For details on searching these, please see the chapter on Lycos.

OTHER FEATURES

Customization

On both the home page and Advanced search page, there is a "Customize" link that enables you to customize the following:

- **Offensive Content Reduction**—An "adult content" filter

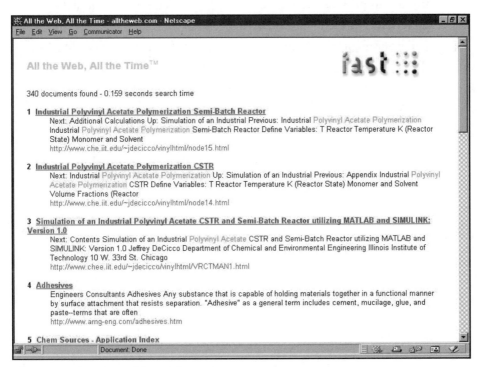

Figure 5.3 Fast Search's results page

- **Language Settings**—This allows you to limit your retrieval to one or more of 47 languages as well as one or more of 21 character sets.
- **Number of Word Filters**—To increase or decrease the number of word-filter boxes shown on the Advanced search page.

All of these can be done individually on the Advanced Search page, as well as by using the Customize link.

SUMMARY OF FAST SEARCH

Fast Search is the newest of the large Web Search engines. Its emphasis is indeed on providing a high-quality retrieval technology that can provide fast and effective access to a maximum-size Web database. The FAST company's emphasis is on the storage and retrieval end of things, and it's positioning itself to leave the mass marketing side of things to partners such as Lycos. Look for Fast Search to become the engine and database behind other services. Its promise to provide the world's largest Web database was a factor in the renewal of the size race. Whether or not it's the largest at a particular moment, it's definitely one of them. So if you're looking for everything on the topic, be sure to include Fast Search for speed and for good relevance ranking all at the same time. Also be sure to put Fast Search on your list of places to search for images.

CHAPTER 6

Google
www.google.com

OVERVIEW

Google is a "popularity" engine and ranks records in its very large database primarily based on their popularity—i.e., the degree to which other pages (especially other popular pages) refer (link) to a page. Google very quickly achieved a widespread popularity of its own due to the effectiveness of this ranking method—and the extreme simplicity of its search interface. Searching options are very limited, with no truncation, moderate field searching, no case-sensitivity, etc. Google retrieves records based on an ANDing of all terms and ranks the output primarily by popularity, but with

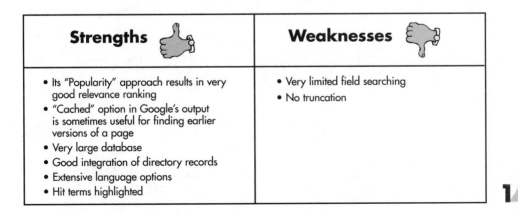

Strengths 👍	Weaknesses 👎
• Its "Popularity" approach results in very good relevance ranking • "Cached" option in Google's output is sometimes useful for finding earlier versions of a page • Very large database • Good integration of directory records • Extensive language options • Hit terms highlighted	• Very limited field searching • No truncation

some consideration for the proximity of search terms within the record. Google has an Advanced Search page that presents the searching options clearly, and does add some substantially increased functionality over the home page version. Google makes use of Open Directory and includes matching Open Directory records automatically in search output, but, unlike other search engines, ranks the Open Directory content based upon Google's measure of popularity. Google's output is unique among the major search engines in that it allows you to go to the page as it's currently on the Web, or to go to a "cached" copy that Google stored when it retrieved the page. Google contains over 1.3 billion records, about half of them fully indexed.

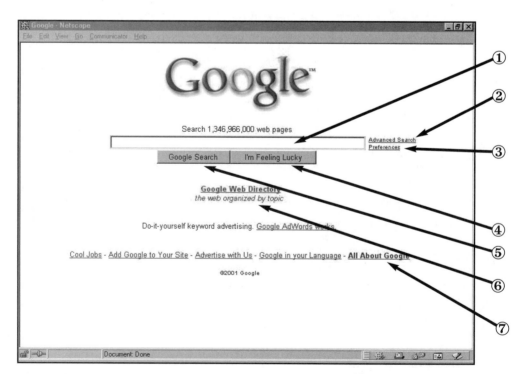

Figure 6.1 Google's home page

GOOGLE'S HOME PAGE

① **Query box**—Enter one or more terms, -term, OR, or field qualifiers. Google will ignore small, very common words unless you insert a plus sign in front of them.

② **Link to Advanced Search**

③ **Link to Language, Display, and Filtering Preferences**—Allows choice of interface language, search language, number of results to be displayed per page, and adult-content filter

④ **I'm Feeling Lucky option**—Will take you directly to the page that Google would have listed first in your results. If you're really lucky, it works.

⑤ **"Google Search" option**—Click to submit your query.

⑥ **Link to Open Directory**—Google has the habit of frequently moving this and other links around on the home page.

⑦ **Help**, etc.

WHAT HAPPENS BEHIND THE SCENES

The key to Google's popularity as a search engine is the pronounced effectiveness of its use of page popularity as a ranking approach. Records are retrieved based on an ANDing of all terms in the query and then the pages are ranked based on the popularity of those pages—i.e., the degree to which other pages (especially other popular pages) refer (link) to a page. Google's brand name for this is PageRank. A measure of "importance" is assigned to a page dependent upon that measure of "popularity" and independent of your current query, although some consideration is indeed given to the proximity of search terms within retrieved records. Google also tracks the font size of text, and the words with larger font size are given greater weight.

About half the records in the Google database are uncrawled sites that Google has identified by their having been linked to by other sites in Google's database. Among these are records from databases that a crawler cannot reach. Google makes this possible because it indexes the words in "anchors" (links) and the associated link. A search on those words can lead you to the linked page. If, for example, a page had a link that led to a record in MEDLINE, crawlers typically cannot reach that record. Since Google indexed the text in the anchor (maybe the article's title or author) and indexed the associated text, it can deliver the MEDLINE record.

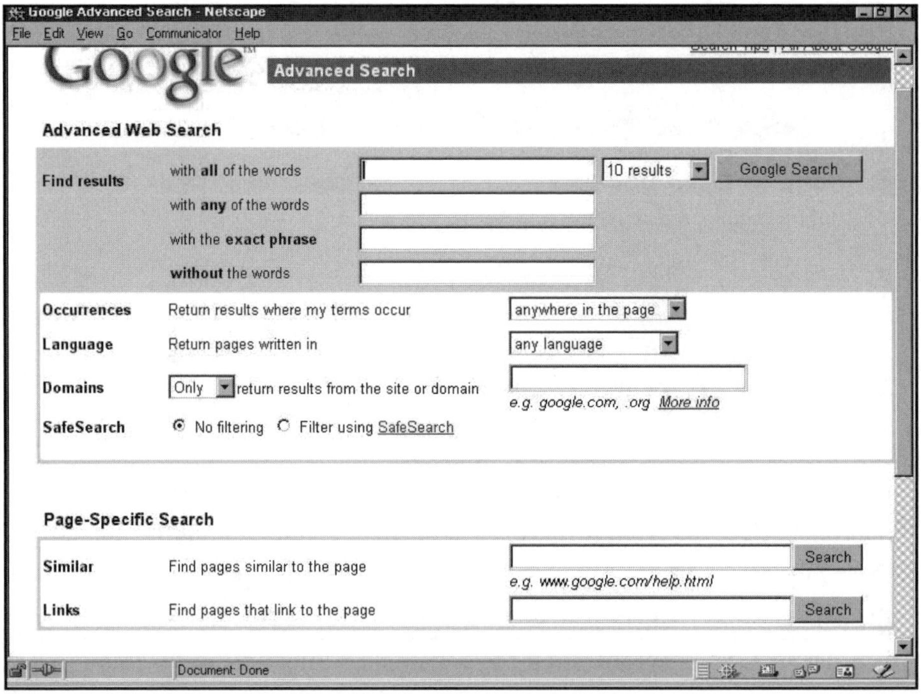

Figure 6.2 Google's Advanced Search page

GOOGLE'S ADVANCED SEARCH

Google's Advanced Search option (see Figure 6.2) provides greater clarity as to what search features can be used. It also provides some increased functionality with title, URL, language, and link searching options, plus a "similar pages" feature and options for the number of results per page.

SEARCH FEATURES

Boolean

Google automatically ANDs all of your words. It also allows ORs and the minus (NOT) operator.

Example: Paris treaty OR treaties −1783

The plus sign can be used, but only has significance when used in front of very small common words that would otherwise be ignored by Google as stop words. (See the discussion that follows under "Phrase Searching.") OR cannot be used with phrases.

Field Searching

Google allows searching by title, URL, site, language, and link.

Title

You can search title in either mode by using the (clunky) allintitle prefix—e.g., allintitle:adderall. Or, you can specify title using the "Occurrences" section of Google's Advanced mode. The latter is easier.

URL

URL can be searched in either mode by using the (equally clunky) allinurl prefix—e.g., allinurl:www.ox.ac.uk. Or, you can specify title using the "Occurrences" section of Google's Advanced mode, which is easier.

Site

The use of the "site" search is very similar to the URL search, but, interestingly, you can (actually, you *must*) use it in combination with a term (for example: biochemistry site:www.nserc.ca).

Language

In Google's Advanced Search version, the following languages are searchable by using the pull-down Languages window:

- Chinese
  (Simplified or Traditional)
- Czech
- Danish
- Dutch
- English

- Estonian
- Finnish
- French
- German
- Greek
- Hebrew
- Hungarian
- Icelandic
- Italian
- Japanese
- Korean
- Latvian
- Lithuanian
- Norwegian
- Polish
- Portuguese
- Romanian
- Russian
- Spanish
- Swedish

The choice of language(s) can also be made on the "Preferences" page, which gives you the choice of more than one language (most search engines only allow for "all languages" or a single language). You can also save those preferences as your default. That page also allows you to have Google display tips and messages in any one of several languages.

Link

In either version of Google, you can find pages that link *to* a particular page by the use of the "link:" prefix in front of the URL.

Example: link:www.jhu.edu

In Advanced mode, you can use the "Find pages that link to the page" option.

Google's link function is less flexible and effective than the equivalent in other search engines. If the address contains a "www," you have to enter it for Google to find the links to it. In neither mode can you combine a link search with other search terms.

Phrase Searching

" "   Phrases can be searched using quotation marks.

If your phrase contains stop words, it gets a little trickier. In that case, you need to put a plus in front of the stop words, although this begs the question of which words Google counts as stop words. Fortunately, when you include a stop word Google responds with a message telling you so. (Among the stop words are *a*, *an*, *are*, *be*, *by*, *com*, *for*, *from*, *I*, *is*, *of*, *to*, *was*, and *with*.) A plus in front of a *non*-stop word will cause all pluses to be ignored. In "to be or not to be" if you put pluses in front of all words it doesn't work, because "not" is not a stop word—but you do need the plus in front of the other words. "Or" gets ignored in any case. Therefore, the solution in Google is to search for

"+to +be or not +to +be"

In general, do your search as you normally would, and if Google tells you some of your words are stop words, go back and insert pluses in front of those words.

Google's handling of stop words can be used to fake a bit of proximity searching. If you have a phrase, but think an additional word might be inserted (and you don't know which word), fake the unknown word using a stop word, such as "by." (I'll use "by" simply because it connotes a sense of proximity.) "Erasmus by Rotterdam" (in quotation marks) would find "Erasmus of Rotterdam," "Erasmus von Rotterdam," Erasmus University Rotterdam," etc. "Erasmus by by Rotterdam" would find others (but fewer), such as "Erasmus University of Rotterdam" because it will insist on two words between. Remember that by inserting a Google stop word, you're insisting that some word be there. You won't necessarily find all those where the words are right next to each other.

Truncation

Google doesn't provide any form of truncation.

Case-Sensitivity

Google is not case-sensitive. However, it is sensitive to diacritics and non-Roman characters, so if you're searching for accented or non-English words, you may achieve better results by the use of the exact character rather than its nearest English equivalent (as you would need to do in many search engines).

Results Pages

Google ranks output by the proximity of your search terms within the record, with some consideration for the proximity of the query terms in the record. Google's output is interesting in that it allows you to go to the page as it's currently on the Web, or to go to a "cached" copy that Google stored when it retrieved the page. To get to the cached copy, click on the "Cached" link. Among other things, this can be useful when you can't find on the current page the terms that retrieved the record. They may have been in the version of the page that was indexed by Google, but do not appear in the current version. It's also useful if the server on which the page resides is temporarily down.

Google delivers 10 results per page as the default, but on the Advanced page you can choose 10, 20, 30, 50, or 100 results per page.

Sample record:

> **Biomedical Engineering Laboratory - HOME (LGM-EPFL)**
> ...activities of the **Biomedical Engineering Laboratory** are...
> ...physics, mechanics and **biomedical engineering**. Location Staff...
> lgmwww.epfl.ch/ - 6k - Cached - Similar pages

Clicking on "Similar Pages" will take you to pages with similar content ("More like this").

If multiple pages are retrieved from the same site, the one judged most relevant will appear first and the next from the same site will be

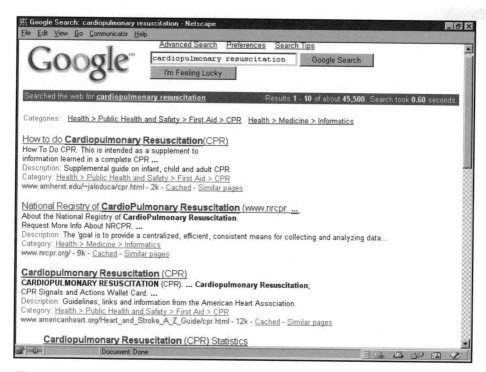

Figure 6.3 Google's results page

listed immediately following, but indented. Additional matches from the site can be seen by clicking on the [More results from …] link.

The text shown in the record just after the title is, unlike with most other search engines, not an "abstract" or description taken from the metatags or first part of the page. Instead you're shown the text surrounding the word(s) that caused the record to be retrieved. To make for easy browsing, Google conveniently highlights the retrieving word(s) by putting them in bold.

In many company, product or service, or brand name searches you'll see an "RN" superscripted next to the company (or other) name—e.g., Oracle Corp. (Oracle[RN]).

This is the link to the record found in the RealNames database and clicking on it will take you directly to the home page of the company (or product, etc.). Whereas some engines (such as AltaVista) will provide a link leading to a list of all entries in the

RealNames database containing the query word, Google only provides the link for a single exact match.

One very impressive feature on search pages receives very little emphasis, but should deserve a lot of the searcher's attention. In the line on the results page where Google reports the number of results, look closely at the search terms that Google has placed in bold and underlined ("cardiopulmonary" and "resuscitation," in the example shown in Figure 6.3). By clicking on such terms you'll be taken to some very useful sources from Dictionary.com, such as extensive dictionary definitions (from The American Heritage Dictionary of the English Language, Webster's Revised Unabridged Dictionary, CancerWEB's On-line Medical Dictionary, and other sources), ZIP codes and geographic descriptions (U.S. Gazetteer), acronym identifications, etc.

Keep an eye out for special content that Google has included in its database. You may, for example, frequently encounter records from the Encyclopaedia Britannica. This type of resource integration can be tremendously valuable.

On the bottom of the results page is a query box with the option to "Search within results." As with other search engines that do a default AND, this is not a big deal. Just sticking an additional term in the box next to the original query will "search within these results" anyway.

As Google has made the inevitable migration from the groves of academe to the commercial fields of battle, it has of course added advertising to its results pages. Mercifully, it has been sticking to text ads with no graphics, which means that results pages can load significantly faster. With ads in general, remember that, in the end, they're what make this amazing degree of information access possible.

DIRECTORY

Google uses Open Directory. It doesn't obviously display the categories on the home page, but provides access by the "Google Web Directory" link. More importantly, perhaps, a search of

Google categories is fully integrated, automatically, into all searches, with matching categories appearing at the top of the results list.

Example:

Results **1-10** of about **988,000** for manitoba. Search took 0.17 seconds.

Category : <u>Regional > North America > Canada > Manitoba > Organizations</u>

Individual site hits from Open Directory are also incorporated into the results list. These can be identified by the presence of a "category" in the record. The same ranking (PageRank) is applied to Open Directory records as to the other results.

To browse the directory, choose the "Google Web Directory" link on the home page. (Google frequently changes what it calls this link.) Google indicates the largest subcategories at each level by putting them in bold. At each level of the directory a search box is provided, and by default Google will search within the current category (unless you choose the "search the Web" option beneath these query boxes). As with search results, when you're browsing the directory, sites are listed by Google's PageRank, but you're also given the option of viewing them alphabetically. Green and gray horizontal bars next to each record indicate the relative popularity of the record.

OTHER SEARCHABLE DATABASES

Periodically, Google features some special databases (which are usually a subset of the main database). For example, Google has offered a government search page, a Linux search page, and a universities search page. Whether these are useful will depend on your specific needs. In each case, ask what the special search is providing that the main Google search is not.

SPECIAL FEATURES

Map Searching

If you enter a U.S. street address (including ZIP code) in the query box, Google will return a link at the top of your results list that will lead you to a map. A street address and city, without the ZIP code, may also work. At present Google provides these through partnerships with providers such as MapQuest.

Stock Search

If a ticker symbol is entered in the query box, the results page will display an option to "Show stock quotes" for that stock. Clicking on that link will take you to the "Excite—Money and Investing" page for that stock. Tabs appear at the top of the page that allow you to receive reports from alternative sources, such as Quote.com.

Adult-Content Filter

Google's adult-content filter, SafeSearch, is provided as an option on the "Preferences" page. It uses a combination of Google's own technology and technology from SurfWatch.

SUMMARY OF GOOGLE

Google provides a deceptively simple interface that, because of the high quality of the ranking mechanism used, quickly gained a reputation for producing high-quality results. Not only will you find good relevance, but because of its enormous database and other factors (such as the way it indexes "anchor" text and links), you will often find things here you won't find elsewhere. It's short on search features, such as truncation, so user control over results is somewhat limited. It very nicely integrates Open Directory content and other resources into its output. Put all of that together and you have a search engine that should and does get heavy usage from all types of searchers—from the infrequent to the incessant.

CHAPTER 7

HotBot
www.hotbot.com

OVERVIEW

HotBot offers a wide variety of search options and presents the most useful ones clearly on its home page. The advanced version presents several more choices. HotBot allows easy field searching, searching by media type (audio, video, etc.), domain, date, etc., as well as full Boolean. The combination of a full range of search options and the fact that the available options are clearly presented make HotBot easy to use, yet powerful enough for both the frequent and infrequent searcher. HotBot is owned by Lycos, and you may see frequent, and probably increasing, overlap and similarities between HotBot's and Lycos' search engine features and services. Though once the largest, HotBot has lost that lead and is now significantly smaller than several other search engines—this is its major weakness.

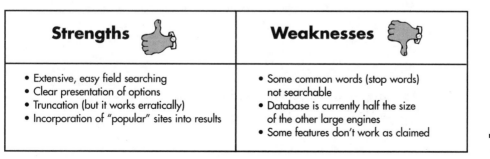

Strengths 👍	Weaknesses 👎
• Extensive, easy field searching • Clear presentation of options • Truncation (but it works erratically) • Incorporation of "popular" sites into results	• Some common words (stop words) not searchable • Database is currently half the size of the other large engines • Some features don't work as claimed

HotBot accesses Inktomi's database of about 500 million pages. Due, however, to HotBot's implementation of this, retrieval numbers often do not reflect such a large size.

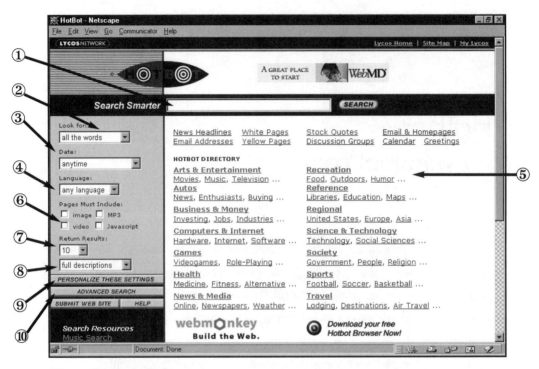

Figure 7.1 HotBot's home page

HotBot's Home Page

① **Query Box**—Can use simple or full Boolean, phrases, etc.

② **Look for:**
- all the words
- any of the words
- the exact phrase
- the page title
- the person
- links to this URL
- Boolean phrase

③ **Date**—In the last week, etc.

④ **Language**—Can choose English, French, Italian, Dutch, German, Spanish, Finnish, Swedish, or Portuguese

⑤ **HotBot's Directory**—Includes special features and links to the Open Directory Web directory

⑥ **Pages Must Include**—image, MP3, video, JavaScript

⑦ **Number of results per page**—With 10, 25, 50, or 100 records

⑧ **Format**—full descriptions   brief descriptions   URLs only

⑨ **Personalize settings**—Can select which search options appear on the page

⑩ **Link to advanced mode**

WHAT HAPPENS BEHIND THE SCENES

HotBot defaults to the AND. Documents that match the search criteria are scored based on the following factors:

- Word frequency in document

- Occurrence of search words in title

- Occurrence of search words as keywords—Terms in the keyword's metatag contribute more to the score than text words, but less than title words.

- Document length—N number of occurrences in a short document rank higher than the same number of terms in a long document.

- Anti-spamming—Various tricks are used by Web page creators to cause a document to receive an artificially high score when examined by search engines. An example would be using a word hundreds of times in a document. If HotBot identifies these, it lowers the score.

HotBot has a list of some common words that are not indexed (stop words). Fortunately, this list has gotten much smaller over time.

Direct Hit—HotBot employs the Direct Hit engine to identify "most popular sites." For common searches, up to 10 of the "most frequently clicked" sites will appear at the top of the results list. **This can be very useful, especially for simple, common topics**—and for finding company home pages.

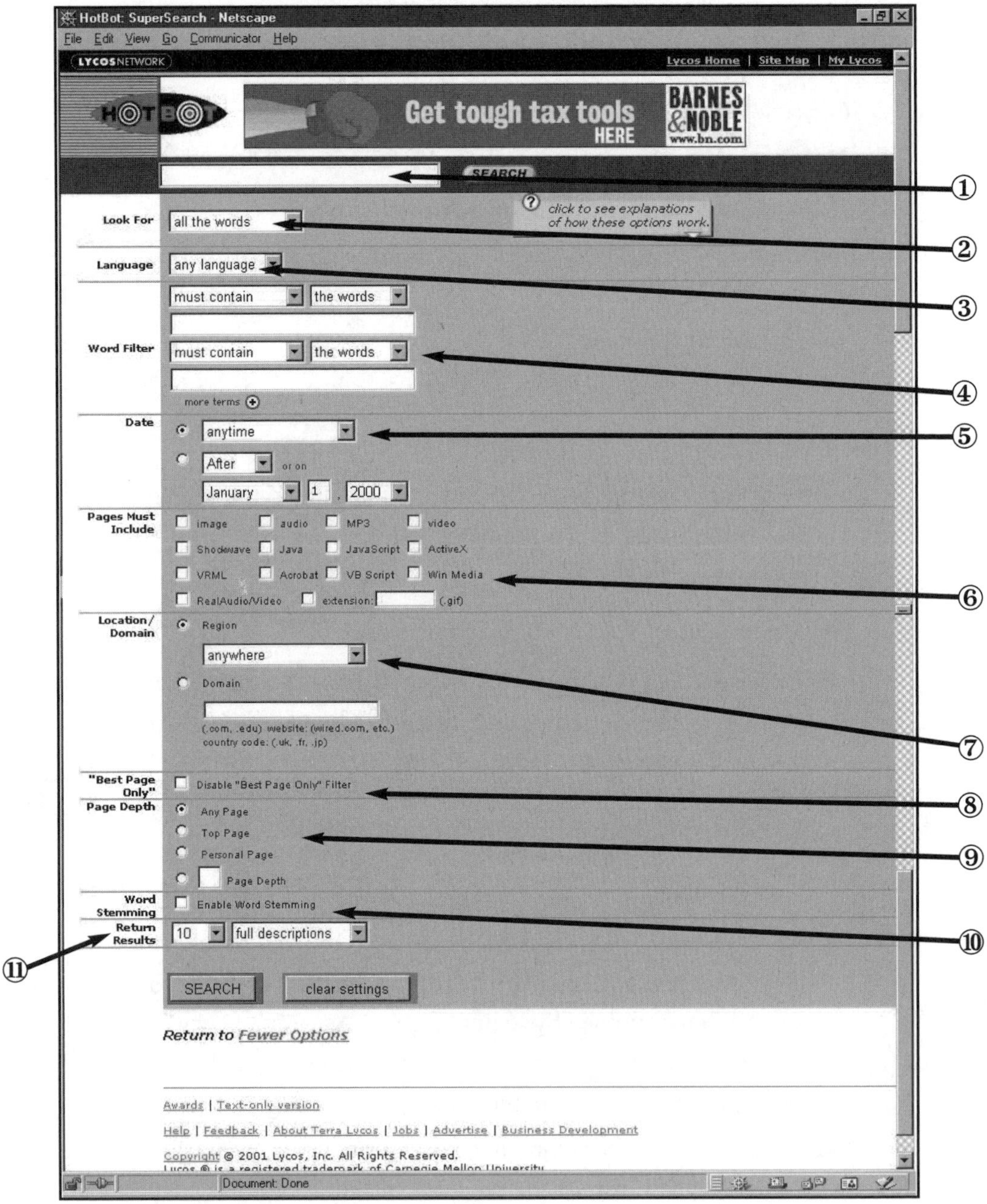

Figure 7.2 HotBot's Advanced Search page

HotBot's Advanced Search

To get to the advanced version, click the "Advanced Search" button on the home page.

HotBot's Advanced Page:

① **Query box**

② **Type of Search** (Look for):

• all the words	• any of the words	• the exact phrase
• the page title	• the person	• links to this URL
• Boolean phrase		

③ **Language**

④ **Modifiers**

- must contain | the words
- should contain | the phrase
- must not contain | the person

⑤ **Date**

Option of specifying "in the last week," etc.

or

After or before a specific date

⑥ **Media**

• Image	• Audio	• MP3 Video	• Video
• Shockwave	• Java	• JavaScript	• ActiveX
• VRML	• Acrobat	• VB Script	• Win Media

⑦ **Location**

Can choose:

Domain (.edu, .com., etc.—period is optional)

or

URL

or

a continent (as in the home page mode)

⑧ **"Best Page Only"**—Option to display one page per Web site

⑨ **Page Depth (type)**

Any page (default) Top page

or

You can specify how many pages "deep" you want
to go (actually specifies how many directory levels
of the URL are permitted)

or

You can limit retrieval to personal pages

⑩ **Word Stemming**—To accept grammatical variations of words

⑪ **Number of results per page**—10, 25, 50, or 100 records **and Format:**

- full descriptions • brief descriptions • URLs only

On the right side of the Advanced Search page, there's a link to "see explanations of how these work." Clicking this will insert a concise explanation beside each of the features.

SEARCH FEATURES

Boolean Logic

Simple Boolean

Simple Boolean can be used in either the home page or Advanced Search version by using the pull-down "Look for" window and putting your terms in the query box. Pluses and minuses can also be used:

- For **AND**, use the **"all the words"** option. This is the default.
- For an **OR**, use the **"any of the words"** option.

When you use pluses and minuses, choose "any of the words" as the "Look for" window option.

Example: [any of the words] +bronxville +restaurant +chinese -cantonese

Advanced Search page—Simple Boolean can be done with the word filter windows, by using the following:

the "must contain" choice for an AND
the "should contain" choice for an OR
the "must not contain" choice for a NOT

Full Boolean

In either version of HotBot, if you want to use full Boolean (AND, OR, NOT) you **must choose the "Boolean phrase" option in the query box.** If you do not, the operators you enter will be ignored.

You can then use: **AND OR NOT ( )**

Example: (merger OR mergers) AND
telecommunications NOT TCI

Field Searching

Of all the Web search engines, HotBot offers one of the best collections of searchable fields, which are searched as shown in Table 7.1.

In addition to searching fields by using the check boxes, radio buttons, and text boxes presented on its interface, HotBot—through the use of prefixes (which HotBot refers to as "meta words")—offers the option of searching fields as part of your term entry in the query box. These prefixes are entered with either "any of the words" or "the Boolean phrase" in the "Look for" box. The list below shows the syntax for searching this way. Each of the prefixes corresponds to one of the fields listed in Table 7.1. The most significant options are covered by the boxes on the search page (and by using those boxes you don't have to worry about syntax). The truly obsessive searcher can use the following examples. The ones in bold are options not available in the panels (i.e., to use them they must be entered as meta words).

HotBot Prefixes

- title:[term]
- domain:[name]
- linkdomain:[name]
- scriptlanguage:[language]
- depth:[number]
- feature:[name]

- title:degas
- domain:mit.edu
- linkdomain:army.mil
- scriptlanguage:javascript
- depth:1
- feature:acrobat

For the feature prefix, [name] in the above can be any of the following: acrobat, activex, **applet**, audio, **embed**, **form**, **frame**, image, **script**, shockwave, **table**, video, vrml.

Example: museum AND feature:shockwave

Table 7.1 Field Searching with HotBot

Field	To search, use:	HotBot	Options/Examples
Date	Date panel	both	"in last week" "in last 2 weeks" "in last month" "in last 3 months" "in last 6 months" "in last year" "in last 2 years"
		Advanced	all of the above plus: (before or after) user- specified date
Title	"Look for" window	both	words in title
Domain	Location/Domain Panel	Advanced	user-specified (.edu,.com, .mil, .net, etc.)
Continent	Location/Domain Panel	Advanced	North America (.net), Europe
URL	Location/Domain Panel	both	ford.com taurus.ford.com (up to three levels)
Language	Language Panel	both	English
Link	"Look for" window	both	Finnish auckland.ac.nz
Media Type	"Pages Must Include" Panel	Advanced	image, audio, video, Shockwave all of the above plus VBScript Acrobat, JavaScript, ActiveX, Java,VRML, .gif, etc. (user specified)
Page Depth	Page Depth panel	Advanced	Any page (default) Top Page Page depth (user specified) Personal Pages

Phrase Searching

Phrases can be searched either by entering the phrase and choosing "the phrase" as the type of search in the "Look for" window, or by using quotation marks around the phrase. Other than exact phrases, proximity searching is not available.

Example: "circuit boards"

Truncation

*   An asterisk is used for truncation.

HotBot provides both user-controlled truncation and the option of automatic word-stemming. In both versions of HotBot, to truncate, use the **asterisk**.

In the advanced version, you have the option of using automatic word stemming by clicking on the "Enable Word Stemming" box. When you do so, HotBot will retrieve some grammatical variations—e.g., "seek" will retrieve "seeking," etc.

Stemming and truncation cannot be used together. In most cases, it will be simpler and probably more effective just to stick to truncation. BUT:

Beware: Truncation in HotBot doesn't work consistently. At times, the left-hand truncation (e.g., *man) described in its documentation did work, making it unique among Web search engines. At times even simple right-hand truncation does not work.

Case-Sensitivity

Though HotBot's documentation claims that it's case-sensitive, the evidence points to the contrary, so don't count on it when you need a case-sensitive search.

Name Searching

When searching for a person's name in the "Look for" box, choose "the person." (However, so that you can copy and paste your entry most effectively into other search engines, capitalize the name appropriately.) When you specify "the person," HotBot automatically searches for the inverted form as well as the normal form of the name.

Example: Winston Churchill will retrieve both:

Winston Churchill

Churchill, Winston

RESULTS PAGES

HotBot displays only one result per site. To see additional pages from a site, click on "See results from this site only" at the end of a record. HotBot will display up to 1,000 results. On the second page of results you'll see an indication of approximately how many total records were retrieved.

As mentioned earlier, HotBot uses Direct Hit's "popularity engine." For searches that are common enough, on results pages you'll see "Top 10 Matches" at the top of the list. These first 10 records are from Direct Hit. If Direct Hit does not have 10 (or if you've modified your query in any way, such as by date), you'll see a link to "Get the Top N sites for 'xxx.'"

For many searches, HotBot results pages will include the following (see Figure 7.3):

- **Suggested alternate searches**—Under "REFINE YOUR SEARCH" or "PEOPLE WHO DID THIS SEARCH ALSO SEARCHED FOR" are some additional searches to consider. Look here for some potentially good ideas about how to modify your search.
- **Related Categories**—From Open Directory
- **Links to Lycos Network resources**—For company searches. Links to stock quotes, charts, SEC filings, financial news, etc. from Quote.com.

- **Top 10 matches**—Direct Hit results (ranked by "popularity")
- **Matching directory records**—From Open Directory ("selected" sites)
- **Web database results**—From the Inktomi database (ranked by relevance)

This combination of "popular," then "selected," then "relevance ranked" records can be very effective in identifying good records quickly.

On results pages, next to the query box, HotBot presents a check box allowing you to specify that you want to search "within these results." Whether you add a word to your query and don't check the box, add a word to your query and do check the box, or check the box and replace what's in the box with your additional term, the results are the same. Here and in some other search engines that provide a similar offering, this may be a

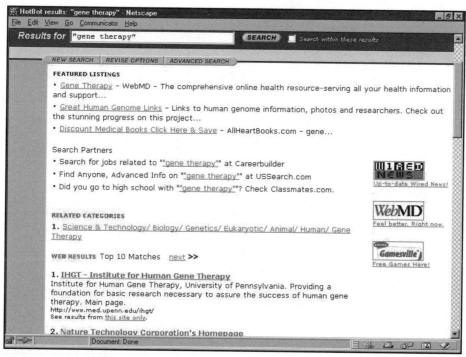

Figure 7.3 HotBot's results page

"much ado about nothing" feature. In any search engine, you can "search within these results" just by adding additional qualifiers to the query.

Full Descriptions:

2. Bioinformatics - Computational Biology

Compendium of Internet-accessible links to bioinformatics centers & institutions, computational biology guides & documentation, software, academic programs and meetings.

http://www.unl.edu/stc-95/ResTools/biotools/biotools4.html

See results from this site only.

Brief Descriptions:

2. Bioinformatics - Computational Biology

Compendium of Internet-accessible links to bioinformatics centers & institutions, computational biology guides & documentation, software, academic programs and meetings.

URLs Only:

2. Bioinformatics - Computational Biology

http://www.unl.edu/stc-95/ResTools/biotools/biotools4.html

HOTBOT'S DIRECTORY

HotBot uses Open Directory for its Web directory. When you click on one of the directory categories listed on HotBot's home page you are accessing Open Directory. HotBot's implementation is fairly standard, and at each level you can search either the entire directory or just within the current level. HotBot makes further effective use of Open Directory by, as discussed above, automatically integrating any sites from the directory into all search results (after the Direct Hit popular results and before the results from the large Inktomi database). In addition to the directory sites being listed within the results, "Related categories" from the directory will be displayed on the first page of results.

SPECIAL OPTIONS/FEATURES

HotBot provides a number of useful add-ons on both its home page and advanced page. In terms of portal features, HotBot should probably not be considered as a general portal in that it does not provide any personalization options or features such as prominently displayed news headlines, weather, and other portal-type offerings found on some other sites. It does, however, provide a good collection of useful links.

Links to Specialized Searches and Other Services

These are found on HotBot's main page and advanced page and include the following, most of which have search engines of their own.

News Headlines	Provides a search of 20 leading news wires and newspapers
Yellow Pages	Powered by GTE Superpages
White Pages	Uses WhoWhere?
Email Addresses	Uses WhoWhere?
Email and Homepages	Links to Mailcity.com and Tripod.com
Calendar	Link to Lycos' Calendar by AnyDay
Greeting cards	Americangreetings.com's free e-mail greeting cards
Lycos SHOP	Goes to the Lycos online shopping site
Free Downloads	The ZDNet download site for software
FTP Search	Goes to the Lycos/Fast Search site for 100 million files for software, MP3s, games, screen-savers, pictures, etc.
Find Alumni	Goes to Classmates.com
Road Maps	Link to MapQuest
Books	Barnes & Noble

Hardware	Goes to the computer section of the Lycos shopping site
Domain Names	Link to the namesecure.com domain name registration site
Classifieds	Goes to a page that links to a variety of HotBot partners such as AutoTrader.com, eBay, Match.com, etc.
Stock Quotes	Quote.com's extensive stock information site
Music Search	Music Boulevard online music store
Jobs & Resumes	A collection of job-related links by The Career Builder Network
Research Service	Provides a link to the Electric Library's subscription service for Magazines, Maps, Books & Reports, Newspapers & Newswires, Transcripts, and Pictures
Travel	Trip.com's travel site
Autos	Link to AutoTrader.com
Auctions	Lycos Auctions site

Page Depth

By using the Page Depth option on HotBot's Advanced page, you can specify that you want just a site's top-level page, or specify how far down in the hierarchy of a site's pages you're willing to go. One application of this would be looking for a company's home page. If, for example, you're looking for the company Biogen, specify "Biogen" as a title word and click on Top Page. It may take you directly to what you want without having to deal with over 100 other pages. (This, however, is one of those features that doesn't always work.)

SUMMARY OF HOTBOT

For the serious searcher, HotBot's features, ease of use, and integration of directory results make it a valuable resource. Its options are clearly laid out so the user knows what's possible. Because of this, HotBot can be productively used by both frequent searchers and occasional searchers. Its greatest weakness is the size of the database, which may have been remedied by the time you read this.

CHAPTER 8

Lycos
www.lycos.com

OVERVIEW

Lycos, one of the earliest Web search engines, had remained fairly stagnant for a long period in terms of size. It had put much more emphasis on its portal nature with an increasingly broad array of added features. With a significant increase in the size of its database in 2000, it now provides a powerful and large search engine in a rich portal context, with the incorporation of a variety of valuable resources into search results. (Much of this size and functionality is attributed to its utilization of the database and search technology provided by Fast Search.) Lycos provides two levels of searching. The Lycos home page version has minimal search features (+word, -word, " "). Lycos Advanced Search provides considerably more

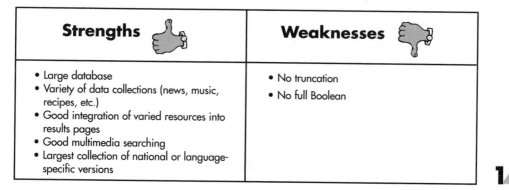

Strengths 👍	Weaknesses 👎
• Large database • Variety of data collections (news, music, recipes, etc.) • Good integration of varied resources into results pages • Good multimedia searching • Largest collection of national or language-specific versions	• No truncation • No full Boolean

139

options, with several searchable fields and a dozen alternative data-bases (such as multimedia and recipes). Lycos is also very interna-tional, with over 30 country/language-specific versions. The Lycos database contains about 575 million pages.

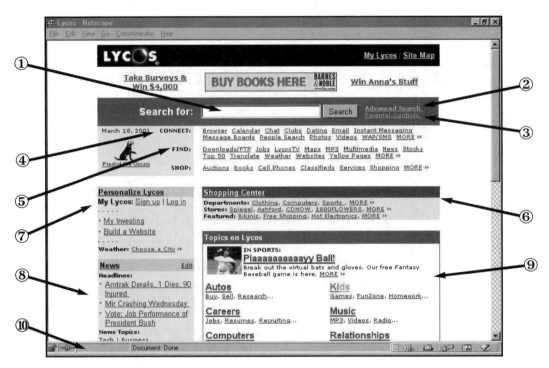

Figure 8.1 Lycos' home page

LYCOS' HOME PAGE

On Lycos' home page you will see the following options:

① **Query box**

> *Simplified* Boolean can be used:

> | | |
> |---|---|
> | **+word** | To AND a term, use a plus sign directly in front of the word. |
> | **-word** | To NOT a term, use a minus sign directly in front of the word. |

> Use " " for phrases

② **Link to "Lycos Advanced Search"**

③   **Parental Controls**—Lycos' adult-content filter

④   **"Connect" Links**—Message boards, calendar, chat, e-mail, free Internet service, instant messenger, translation program, etc.

⑤   **Find Links**—(searchable databases, etc.) Downloads, FTP, Jobs (classifieds), TV listings, Maps, MP3, News, People (White Pages), Multimedia, Stocks, Top 50 (Lycos searches), Video, Weather, Websites (Open Directory), Yellow Pages

⑥   **Shopping Links**

⑦   **Personalization (Customization) option**—My Lycos

⑧   **Headlines**

⑨   **Lycos Topics and Web Directory**

⑩   **Non-U.S. versions**—Links are below the area shown

What Happens Behind the Scenes

Lycos indexes all of the visible words on the page, including small words such as "the" and "a." In simple search mode, when a string of terms is entered, all terms are automatically ANDed. Lycos uses the Fast Search database and retrieval technology. A very important part of what happens behind the scenes is the automatic integration and display of results from various sources (popularity engine, Open Directory categories, Open Directory sites, news) in addition to the sites from the main Web database.

Lycos' Advanced Search

In Lycos' Advanced Search, you're fully using the Fast Search database as well as Fast Search retrieval technology. Functionality is basically the same as with Fast Search itself, but with a modified interface.

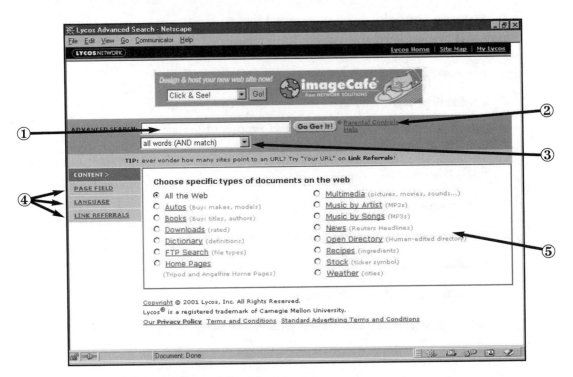

Figure 8.2 Lycos' Advanced Search page

The Lycos Advanced page presents the following options:

① **Query Box**

    +term To AND a term, use a plus sign directly in front of the word.

    -term To NOT a term, use a minus sign directly in front of the word.

    " " Quotation marks for phrases

② **Parental Control Filter**

③ **Search Qualifier Window—Boolean searching is accomplished by the following choices:**

- All the Words (the **default**, equal to an AND)
- Any of the Words (equal to an OR)
- The Exact Phrase

④　**Links to:**

- **Page Field window**—For searching **Title, URL, Host/Domain fields**
- **Language window**—Choice of 25 languages
- **Link Referrals**—For link-to searching

⑤　**Content Window**—To select database/document type to be searched

- All the Web
- Autos
- Books
- Downloads
- Dictionary
- FTP Search
- Home pages
- Multimedia
- Music by Artist
- Music by Songs
- News
- Open Directory
- Recipes
- Stock
- Weather

SEARCH FEATURES

Boolean Logic

Lycos only provides a simplified Boolean option.

Lycos Home:

+term	To AND a term, use a plus sign directly in front of the word.
-term	To NOT a term, use a minus sign directly in front of the word.

The pluses are not really necessary, since Lycos automatically ANDs all terms anyway.

Lycos Advanced

The above, plus window options for:

- All the Words [the default]
- Any of the Words
- The Exact Phrase

Field Searching

Lycos has substantial field searching capabilities in its **Advanced version**, allowing searching by **language**, **title**, **URL**, and **links** (see Figure 8.2). They can be accessed by using the three tabs on the left of the screen (PAGE FIELD, LANGUAGE, LINK REFER-RALS). The fields can also be searched by using prefixes. If you use the tabs, you're more limited in being able to combine fields, since in a single search you can only use one of the tabs. With prefixes you can do more combinations of fields.

Page Field tab:

For searching Title, URL, Host/Domain fields, place terms in the appropriate boxes.

Language tab:

Using the radio buttons, choose from the following 25 languages (to search all languages, do not use this tab):

• Bulgarian	• Icelandic
• Catalan	• Italian
• Czech	• Latvian
• Danish	• Lithuanian
• Dutch	• Norwegian
• English	• Polish
• Estonian	• Portuguese
• Finnish	• Romanian
• French	• Russian
• German	• Slovenian
• Greek	• Spanish
• Hebrew	• Swedish
• Hungarian	

Link Referrals tab—For link-to searching

Using the Link Referrals tab, put the URL of interest in the "Your URL" box. Of course, it doesn't really have to be "your" URL. Remember that this will identify those pages that link to the URL you choose.

Searching Fields in Lycos by Using Prefixes (Advanced Search only):

Title t:

Use the t: prefix and the term.

Examples:

> t:merovingian
>
> t:"merovingian art"

Language l:

Use the l: prefix and the first three letters of the language as listed above.

> *Example:* (for German)
>
> l:ger

URL u:

Use the u: prefix and any contiguous parts of the URL.

> *Examples:*
>
> u:de
>
> u:bayer.de
>
> u:presse-bayer.de

"Links to" ml:

Use the ml: prefix and any contiguous parts of the URL to find sites that link to a particular site.

> *Examples:*
>
> ml:infotoday.com

Host/Domain can also be searched using the **h:** prefix, but the same results can be achieved with the u: prefix.

These can be used in combination. (Choose "all words" in the pull-down window.)

> *Example* (for pages with aspirin in the title, from the
> Bayer site and in German):
>
> t:aspirin u:bayer.de l:ger

Phrase Searching

" " Use quotation marks for a phrase (available in both versions of Lycos).

> *Example:* "medical devices"

Truncation

Truncation is not available in either version of Lycos.

Case-Sensitivity

Lycos is not case-sensitive and cannot distinguish between "Frank" and "frank."

RESULTS PAGES

Lycos nicely integrates several resources into results pages beyond just the matching pages from the Lycos Web database (see Figure 8.3). Narrow searches may retrieve only Web pages, but broader searches are likely to result in a page that contains many of the following:

- **Company information** (from Quote.com)
- **Related Searches** ("People who did this search also searched for")
- **Popular sites** section (containing sites selected on the basis of "user selection traffic"). This may also include special resources, such as links to entries from Infoplease.com Almanac.
- **Web sites** section, which may include:
  1. Matching categories from Open Directory
  2. Matching sites from Open Directory (These can be identified by the category hierarchy—e.g., Society > History > Science—at the bottom of the record, instead of a URL.)
  3. Sites from the Lycos catalog
- Matching **news articles** section
- **Shopping** sites section

Sample Web site record:

> 25. Michel **Foucault** (1926-1984) - Michel **Foucault** (1926-1984) **Foucault**, Michel (1926-1984), French philosopher, who attempted to show that the basic ideas which people normally take to be permanent truths about human nature and society
> http://www.connect.net/ron/foucault.html
> [Translate]

Query terms within records are highlighted.

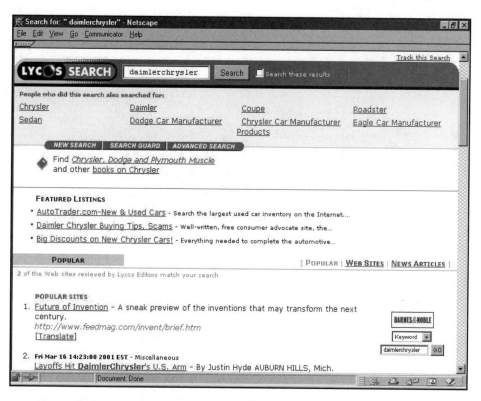

Figure 8.3 Lycos' results page

LYCOS' DIRECTORY

Like several other large Web search services, Lycos uses Open Directory as its Web directory. It's accessible both by browsing from the Lycos home page and also via the ways in which Lycos automatically integrates a search of Open Directory into Web search results pages, displaying, in the latter case, both matching categories and individual matching sites.

When browsing the directory from the home page, on many directory pages Lycos adds links to related Lycos channel pages and resources. On all directory pages, at all levels, Lycos presents a query box with the option of searching the Web, searching the top current-level Open Directory category (e.g., Health), or searching the current subcategory, no matter how far down the hierarchy.

OTHER SEARCHABLE DATABASES

Pictures and Sounds

Lycos provides one of the most straightforward and easy-to-use image and sound searching facilities. Though you can search these using the Advanced Options on Lycos Advanced Search page, you can also use the "Multimedia" link on the home page.

Clicking on the Multimedia link on Lycos' home page will lead to a search page for Pictures, Audio, and Video. This page represents a nice refinement of the Multimedia option on Lycos' Advanced Search page. In addition, Lycos provides a section on the Multimedia page for downloading a wide range of media applications files for use with the search results. The adult-content filtering option (Parental Controls) is also available on this page.

In either interface you can search using simple Boolean (+term, -term) and quotation marks for phrases. For images, the file name, URL, and HTML title are being searched.

Image-results pages show the image size (in pixels) and the file size. Clicking on the image or on the "full-size photo" link under the picture will lead to a screen with the full-size image (alone). In the case of images from the commercial collections indexed by Lycos, information on purchasing rights to use the image will also be shown.

Additional databases searchable through the Advanced Search page

Using the radio button choices on the Advanced Search page, you can search the following databases:

- Autos—Autoweb.com
- Books—Barnes & Noble
- Downloads
- Dictionary—Information Please almanacs, dictionaries, etc.
- FTP Search—Fast Search's FTP search
- Home Pages—Tripod and Angelfire Home Pages
- Multimedia—see above
- Music—MP3s
- News—Reuters
- Open Directory

- Recipes—Lycos' Recipedia collection of recipe sources
- Stocks—Quote.com
- Weather—City forecasts (worldwide)

PORTAL AND PERSONALIZATION FEATURES

Personalization ("My Lycos")

You can personalize these sections of the Lycos home page:

- **News headlines**—Your choice of categories; local news by state
- **Stocks**—Choice of stocks and/or indices; a portfolio service
- **Favorite links**—Like bookmarks
- **Local weather**
- **Local sports scores**
- **A variety of other portal features**

Channels (Topics)

Though they're given only moderate prominence on the home page, Lycos provides a good collection of channels, which it refers to as "topics." Each of these includes a variety of tools, specialized databases, topic-specific news, downloads, etc. These channels include the following:

- Autos
- Banking
- Books
- College
- Computers
- Entertainment
- Finance
- Free Games
- Health
- Kids
- Music
- Small Business
- Sports
- Travel

Beneath this listing, under "Also," are the Open Directory categories.

Track Your Searches

This is a free **alerting service** that will automatically alert you (via e-mail) to new popular **sites**, **news articles**, or **shopping** items that mention your terms. Unfortunately, you must set up a MailCity (Lycos' free e-mail service) account to be able to receive the alerts.

Click the "Track This Search" link on results pages to set up an alert.

Adult-Content Filter

By means of the Parental Controls link on the Lycos home page, you can choose to have a password-controlled adult-content filter applied. It's customizable (you can select the categories of content to be blocked).

OTHER PORTAL FEATURES

The following are presented on Lycos' home page beneath the query box and elsewhere:

- Auctions—Online auctions
- Calendar—Personal calendar/organizer from AnyDay.com
- Chat—What you'd expect
- Clubs—Online clubs, chat rooms, and message boards
- Ecards—Free electronic greeting cards
- Email—Free e-mail from MailCity
- Home Pages—Free home pages from either Tripod or Angelfire
- Horoscopes
- Instant Messenger—Powered by AOL
- Lycos 50—A usually depressing look at the most frequently performed searches
- Maps—Powered by MapBlast
- Message Boards—Bulletin Boards
- Mobile Access and Services
- MP3—Search engine for over 500,000 MP3 files

- People—WhoWhere? for phone numbers, addresses, e-mail, government officials, travel directions, and international phone directories
- Pictures—The pictures portion of Lycos' multimedia search
- Stocks—Stock quotes and market news using Quote.com (personalizable)
- Yellow Pages—GTE Superpages
- News—Reuters and other news options
- Weather—City-specific weather forecast (personalizable)
- Books—Barnes & Noble
- Music—Lycos' Music channel

The presence of a number of these is a reflection of the corporate holdings of the overall Lycos network, which owns, in addition to the Lycos search engine, the free Web sites Tripod and Angelfire, the WhoWhere? directory, MailCity, HotBot, HotWired, Wired News, Webmonkey, and other properties.

Click on the "More" link in the "Connect," "Find," or "Shop" sections of the home page for an excellent site map that shows all of the Lycos offerings.

International Sites

Through both internal development and partnerships, Lycos presents the greatest number of country- and language-specific sites of all the major search engine services. Most of these interfaces have a very similar appearance to the main interface but are in the native language and with often scaled-down, though sometimes enhanced, offerings. These include:

- Austria
- Argentina
- Belgium
- Brazil
- Canada
- Chile
- China
- Colombia
- Denmark
- France
- Germany
- Hong Kong
- India
- Indonesia

- Italy
- Japan
- Korea
- Malaysia
- Mexico
- Netherlands
- Norway
- Peru
- Philippines
- Singapore

- Spain
- Sweden
- Switzerland
- Taiwan
- Thailand
- U.K.
- Venezuela
- Estados Unidos (An interface for Spanish-speaking Americans)
- Terra (South American partner)

Translations

Lycos offers translations using the SYSTRAN software. If you click on the Translate link under "Find" on the home page, you will be presented with the SYSTRAN page that allows you to enter text (about 40 lines) and translate it between English and French, German, Italian, Portuguese, Russian, or Spanish; or Russian to French; German to French; or French to German. On results pages, you will also see a translate link that enables you to translate the Web pages.

SUMMARY OF LYCOS

Lycos, though not the strongest search engine, does provide a very large database and a good, but not outstanding, collection of search features. (Much of its searching strength is due to its partnership with Fast Search.) Its lack of truncation and case-sensitivity is a drawback. Lycos is very strong on international interfaces, a situation likely to be further enhanced due to Lycos' being owned by Terra Networks, S.A, the leading Internet company in Spanish- and Portuguese-speaking countries. Perhaps Lycos' greatest strength lies in its incorporation of significantly more than just Web database results into its results pages, particularly its integration of Open Directory, news, and other resources. That integration and its collection of specialized databases (images, sounds, recipes, etc.) means that the serious searcher should be sure to be acquainted with Lycos.

CHAPTER 9

Northern Light
www.northernlight.com or www.nlsearch.com

OVERVIEW

Of all the major Web search engines, Northern Light is the only one that focuses its efforts primarily on providing a resource for the serious researcher. In terms of functionality and content, its uniqueness lies in (1) its coverage of proprietary publications (Special Collection) as well as the Web, and (2) its organization of results into customized folders. For the proprietary material, abstracts are provided free and the full text can be purchased by credit card or subscription. This material covers all subjects areas and includes over 7,000 magazines, journals, books, newspapers,

Strengths 👍	Weaknesses 👎
• Straightforward, easy-to-use interface • Searches proprietary as well as Web content • Analyzes and organizes results by "folders" • Excellent field searching • Case-sensitive • Variety of search interfaces, including unique geographic search	• Does not make use of metatags in calculating relevance of records

newsletters, pamphlets, and news wires. When a search is done, Northern Light groups the results into "Custom Search Folders." These folders bring together those results that have common characteristics, such as subject category, type of document, etc. Northern Light has a broad range of search functionality, including extensive field searching capability. The Power Search version provides additional functionality and makes the various options more apparent by means of check boxes and windows. Other "Search Forms" (Business, Investext, News, Stock Quotes, GeoSearch) provide a search focus on those specific areas. With its proprietary information resources, Northern Light is not just a Web search service, but a bibliographic search service and a document delivery service as well.

Northern Light's database includes over 360 million Web pages and over 25 million proprietary articles.

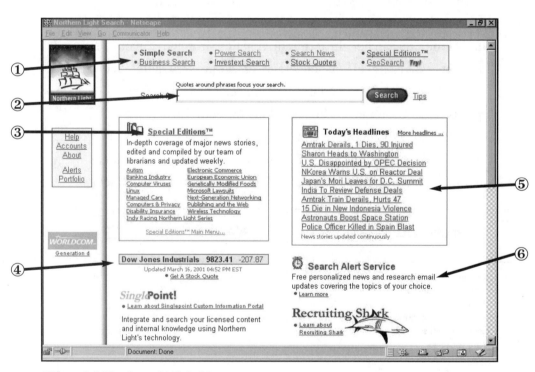

Figure 9.1 Northern Light's home page

NORTHERN LIGHT'S HOME PAGE

① **Links to** Power Search, Business Search, Investext Search, Stock Quotes, News, GeoSearch

② **Query Box** (where Boolean, field searching, etc. can be used)

③ **Special Editions**—Prepackaged links on current hot topics

④ **Dow Jones Industrials report**

⑤ **Today's Headlines**

⑥ **Site promotions**—Actually some very straightforward, informative looks at Northern Light offerings

WHAT HAPPENS BEHIND THE SCENES

Northern Light indexes every word contained in a page and every page of a Web site. The text of proprietary documents is likewise fully indexed. Northern Light retains information on document source, type, subject, and language, which is used for the creation of the Custom Search Folders. As part of that process, Northern Light automatically classifies virtually every document, using a controlled vocabulary that "recognizes several hundreds of thousands of concepts." If you have not specified an AND, OR, or NOT, Northern Light will retrieve those records that contain "most of the words in your search." This allows for "natural language" input such as "Was 1998 a good year for Bordeaux wines?" Northern Light will ignore the more common words in terms of which records are retrieved, but may make use of those words in determining the relevance ranking. Relevancy is calculated based on several factors, including occurrences of query terms and the presence of query terms in document titles. Results are listed according to that relevancy determination.

Northern Light, unfortunately, does not make use of metatags in calculating the relevance of a record.

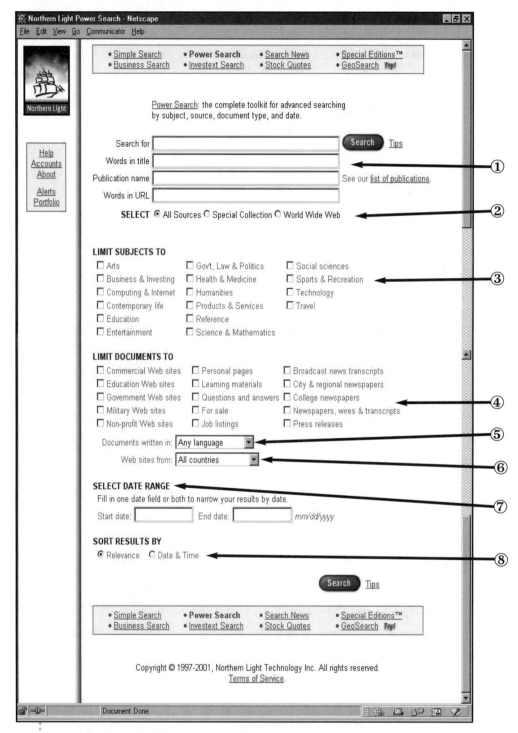

Figure 9.2 Northern Light's Power Search page

NORTHERN LIGHT'S POWER SEARCH

Northern Light Power Search Page Features

① **Query boxes**, which allow searching in **all fields** or **title field, publication name**, or **URL**

② **Choice of Searching:**

- All Sources (World Wide Web and Special Collection)
- World Wide Web
- Special Collection

③ **Limit Subjects To:**

- Arts
- Business & Investing
- Computing & Internet
- Contemporary Life
- Education
- Entertainment
- Government, Law & Politics
- Health & Medicine
- Humanities
- Products & Services
- Reference
- Science & Mathematics
- Social Sciences
- Sports & Recreation
- Technology
- Travel

④ **Limit Documents To:**

- Commercial Web sites
- Education Web sites
- Government Web sites
- Military Web sites
- Non-profit Web sites
- Personal pages
- Learning materials
- Questions and answers
- For sale
- Job listings
- Broadcast news transcripts
- City & regional newspapers
- College newspapers
- Newspapers, wires & transcripts
- Press releases

⑤ **Language** (All, English, French, German, Italian, Spanish)

⑥ **Web sites from (country)**—All or any one of 25 countries

⑦ **Select Date Range**

⑧ **Sort Results By:**

- Relevance
- Date & Time

SEARCH FEATURES

Boolean Logic

Either simplified or full Boolean can be used in Northern Light's "Search for" query boxes on the Simple, Power, Business, Investext, and Geo (geographic location) search forms, and in the main query box on the News Search form.

Simplified Boolean:

+term   To AND a term, use a plus sign directly in front of the word or phrase

-term   To NOT a term, use a minus sign directly in front of the word or phrase

Example:

+"hydrogen peroxide" +production +France

Full Boolean:

AND

OR

NOT (you can also use AND NOT)

( )

Example:

(bison OR buffalo) AND brucellosis
AND transmission

Field Searching

Northern Light provides the most extensive field searching capability of all the Web search engines. It has the capability of searching Web pages by **title, URL, date, subject category, document type, language, country, industry, address,** and **text** words. It can also search various parts of its special collection by **ticker symbol, publication name, research firm, document length,** and **region.** The only fairly common, searchable field that Northern Light does not provide is link searching (for pages linked to a particular page).

URL

This is searchable in Northern Light's Simple, Power, Business, and Geo search forms.

In these forms, you can use the *url:* prefix in the "Search for" box to look for words occurring in the URL.

Examples:

> url:simmons.edu
>
> url:earth.simmons.edu
>
> url:simmons.edu/archives

In Power Search mode, you can search by URL by entering the URL, or segments of it, in the "Words in URL" box.

Title

This is searchable in Northern Light's Simple, Power, Business, Investext, News, and Geo search forms.

In these forms, you can use the *title:* prefix to specify *title* words or phrases.

Example:

> title:ceramics
>
> title:"ceramic tiles"

In Power, Business, and Investext search forms, enter the terms in the "Words in title" box.

Date

Specific date ranges are searchable on the Power, Business, and Investext search pages. A start date and/or an end date can be entered in the Select Date Range boxes using the format, mm/dd/yy.

Example: 04/21/01

On the Power, Business, Investext, and News Search pages, results can also be *sorted* by date. Click the "Date & Time" button under "SORT RESULTS BY."

On the News Search form, you can specify "Last Two Hours," "Today's News," or "Last Two Weeks."

Subject Category

On the Power Search form, you can specify, by using the "Limit Subjects To" check boxes, one or more of the following subject categories:

- Arts
- Business & Investing
- Computing & Internet
- Contemporary Life
- Education
- Entertainment
- Government, Law & Politics
- Health & Medicine
- Humanities
- Products & Services
- Reference
- Science & Mathematics
- Social Sciences
- Sports & Recreation
- Technology
- Travel

Publication

This is searchable in Northern Light's Simple, Power, GeoSearch, and Business search forms and applies only to the Special Collection items (though it may also retrieve Web-based articles from Fortune Online and U.S. Government reports).

Publication titles (such as American Mathematical Monthly), or words from titles, can be searched on the Simple, Power, Business, News, and Geo search forms using the *pub:* prefix in the "Search for" box.

Example: pub:"Agricultural History"

Publication titles can also be searched on the Power and Business search forms by using the "Publication name" box.

Company Name

This is searchable in Northern Light's Simple, Power, Business, Investext, and News search forms. Records retrieved by searching this field will come only from Northern Light's Special Collection.

In these forms, you can use the *company*: prefix to specify title words or phrases.

Example: company:"General Motors"

In Business and Investext search forms, enter the terms in the "Company name" box.

Ticker

This is searchable in all of Northern Light's search forms except GeoSearch. Records retrieved by searching this field will come only from Northern Light's Special Collection.

To search for a company using the ticker symbol in any Northern Light search form (except Quotes and GeoSearch), use the *ticker*: prefix.

Example: ticker:bur

In the Quotes search form, enter just the ticker symbol in the query box.

Text

Use of the text prefix is necessary when entering a Boolean expression that is a combination text and field search. If the prefix is not used, the "text" word may only be searched in the field you just specified. This can be used in all Northern Light search forms except Quotes.

Examples: text:apparel

url:fiba.net AND text:economic

Industry

The Industry "field" is searchable using check boxes on the Business or Investext search forms. From the list of industries, one or more industries or "All Industries" can be selected.

Document Type

In Power, Business, and Investext search forms, results can be limited to the kind of document. Which document choices are available depends on the particular search form. Multiple document types can be chosen.

Searching by document type is made possible by artificial intelligence programs that recognize document types (such as recipes, interviews, etc.) by the general form and other characteristics of the particular type of document.

When searching for a phrase using the prefixes for any of the above fields, use double quotation marks around the phrase. If you don't, the words you enter will be ANDed.

Example: pub: "Health Management"

Phrase Searching

Use double quotation marks to search for phrases. No other proximity options are available.

Truncation

Northern Light automatically stems most common plurals and singulars. A search on "horse" will also retrieve all of the "horses" records.

Northern Light also provides extensive user-controlled truncation (wild card) capability:

* * for right-hand truncation

    Example: comput*

* % The percent sign is used for substituting a single character and can be used for embedded truncation

    Example: workm%n

The % can be used more than once in a term, and the * and % can be used in the same term. A minimum of four initial characters is required (i.e., you can search for tech*, but tec* will not work).

When Northern Light does its relevance ranking, it will not take into consideration those words that were retrieved by use of the wild cards. If the stem you used is a word in itself, that word will be ranked. For example, if you searched for computer*, the word "computer" will factor into the ranking, whereas those with the word "computerization" will not.

Case-Sensitivity

Northern Light is case-sensitive but treats it differently than most search engines. If you search for "Frank," "frank" will also be retrieved, but the "Frank" records (records with matching case) will appear in the results ahead of the ones without matching case.

RESULTS PAGES

Northern Light offers one output format and displays 10 results per page. Results are "grouped" and only the first record from each site (or publication, if from the Special Collection) will be shown. Additional matching sites can be seen by clicking on the "More results from this site" link.

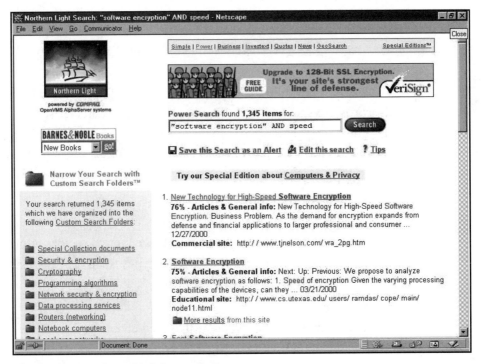

Figure 9.3 Northern Light's results page

Sample Web record:

1. <u>The Project Gutenberg Etext of The Cash Boy by Horatio Alger Jr</u>

   99% - **Articles & General info**: Please take a look at the important information in this header. We encourage you to keep this file on your own disk, keeping an electronic... 01/21/1999

   Commercial site: http://www.usastores.com/gdl/text/cashb10.txt

   📁 More results from this site

Sample Special Collection record:

1. *Special Collection* <u>The Dead Sea Scrolls: translated and with commentary</u>

   78% - **Articles & General info**: The Dead Sea Scrolls: translated and with commentary Michael Wise, Martin Abegg and Edward Cook Harper/Collins, San Francisco 1996 XIV-513 pages; ISBN 0... 04/01/1998

   Mankind Quarterly (magazine): Available at Northern Light

Proprietary (pay-per-view) documents are clearly indicated by the words "Special Collection."

Custom Search Folders

Custom Search Folders are Northern Light's unique way of organizing results. When records are retrieved, they are listed by relevance on the right side of the page, but they're also organized into a selection of topic folders. These folders are created "on the fly," and records are grouped according to the unique characteristics of the particular search. Northern Light identifies "topics" common to various of the retrieved records and creates folders for those topics. In creating these folders, over 30 document types and 15,000 subject classifications are used.

In addition to subject folders, folders may also be created for:

- Type of document (such as press releases, maps, recipes, etc.)
- Source (by domain type or source types such as personal pages, magazines, encyclopedias, etc.)
- Language

An added benefit of the folders is that they enable you to *narrow* the results of your current search. When you click on one of the folders, the contents of that folder are divided into a new set of folders.

You cannot search within a particular folder, but you can have the system narrow the results by creating the new set of categories.

For a search on "software encryption," the folders created are shown in Figure 9.3.

DIRECTORY

Since its beginning, Northern Light has been automatically classifying, by subject heading, a large portion of the pages it indexes. These subject headings in the past were only visible by their presence as the topics of the Custom Search Folders. It is now compiling them into a browsable, hierarchical directory, which is accessible and browsable from Northern Light's home page. This directory contains approximately 60 million items, making it over 20 times as large as competing directories like Open Directory and Yahoo! Keep in mind, though, that traditional directories (Yahoo!, Open Directory, LookSmart, and others) are characterized not just by the classification of sites, but by human selectivity—every site in those directories has been checked by an editor to determine its appropriateness for the directory.

Although Northern Light's directory is many times larger, it does not reflect the selectivity that the others provide. Partially compensating for this is the fact that the listing of sites within each category is in order of popularity (measured by the number of Web pages that link to that page). This aspect does introduce a degree of the subjectivity/selectivity characteristic of traditional Web directories.

Within each level of the hierarchy, you can also perform a "search," limiting your retrieval to only items found within that category.

SPECIAL OPTIONS AND "SEARCH FORMS"

In addition to the Simple and Power search modes ("forms"), Northern Light also offers special search forms for Business, Investext, Stocks, News, Quotes, and Geo (geographic location). To get to any of the search forms, click the corresponding link found at the top or bottom of virtually any Northern Light page. It also presents an automatic

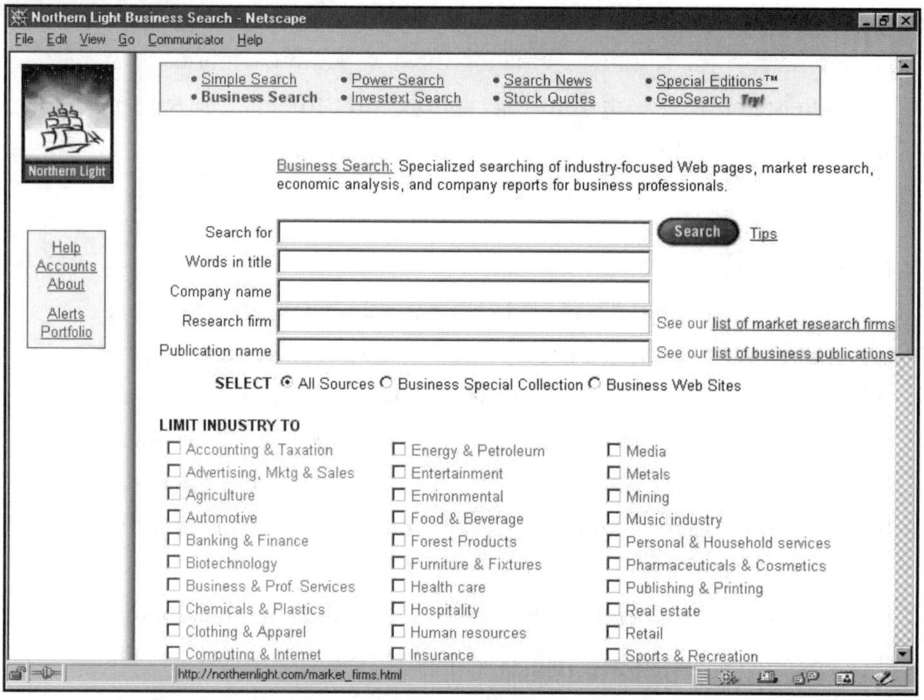

Figure 9.4 Northern Light's Business Search page

alerting service and a collection of "Special Edition" resource pages. The proprietary collection is, of course, one of Northern Light's most outstanding and unique features.

Business Search

The Business Search form provides access to business- and industry-related material, market research, economic analysis, and company reports drawn from both Northern Light's Web database and Special Collection.

In addition to subject searching in the "Search for" query box, the Business Search form provides the following search capabilities:

- Title searching
- Company name searching (applies only to the Special Collection)
- Research firm (help screens provide a list of the approximately 100 market research firms)

- Publication name (applies only to the Special Collection)
- Limiting to the business portion of the Special Collection or Business Web sites (default is "All Sources")
- Limiting to specific industry or industries, from a list of 41 industries (see Figure 9.4). Northern Light's help screens give the description used for each industry.
- Limiting to Document type—Specify one of several leading business publications and/or type of document
- Selecting Date Range—Specify start/end dates using the mm/dd/yyyy format.
- Sorting results—You can choose to sort by date and time, instead of the default relevance order.

Investext Search

This collection includes reports from brokerage houses and investment banks, as well as research firms from around the world. On Northern Light, the Investext collection goes back to January 1997.

In addition to subject searching in the "Search for" query box, the Investext search form provides:

- Title searching
- Company name searching
- Searching by ticker symbol
- Research firm
- Display of results by Report or Page—Keep in mind that Investext reports can be very lengthy and for broad topics you may want to see just a list of reports before seeing a list of all pages.
- Limiting to specific industry or industries, from a list of 29 industries (see Figure 9.5)—By clicking on the name of the industry, you can browse without specifying a subject. Reports are listed most recent first. Northern Light's help screens give the description used for each industry.
- Limiting by document length—Small (1-5 pages), Medium (6-49 pages), or Large (50 or more pages)

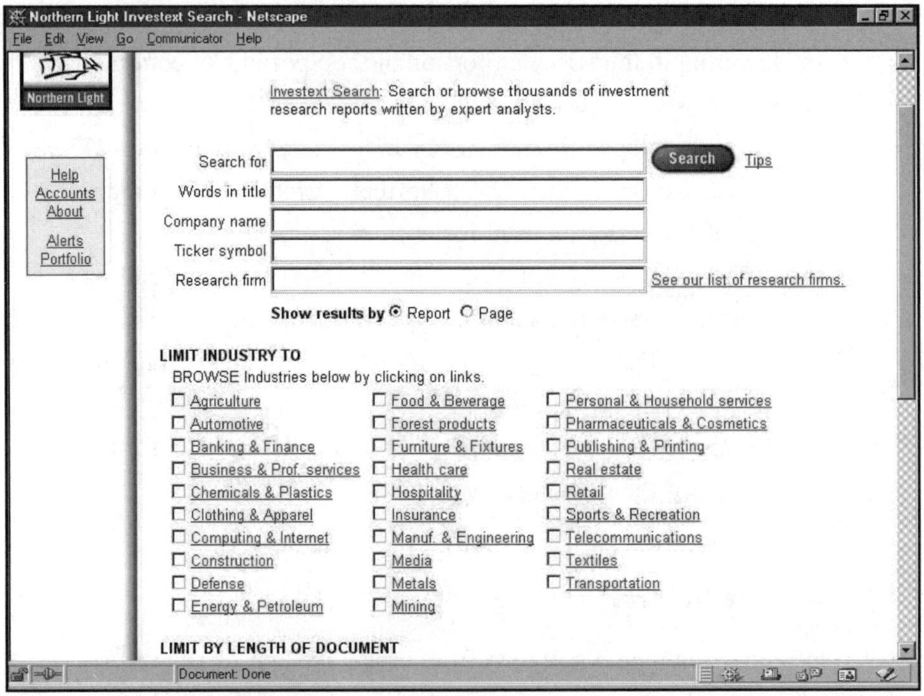

Figure 9.5 Northern Light's Investext Search page

- Limiting by Region
- Limiting to Company reports or Industry reports
- Selecting Date Range—Specify start/end dates using the mm/dd/yyyy format.
- Sorting results—You can choose to sort by date and time, instead of the default relevance order.

Stock Quotes Search

This interface allows a stock lookup by ticker symbol for stocks traded on the NASDAQ and New York Stock Exchanges. A link to the right of the query box provides a symbol lookup if you know the name of the company but not the symbol. The search page itself provides an intraday performance graph of the Dow Jones Industrial Average and for NASDAQ, plus reports on other major indices (see Figure 9.6).

Results pages include a 20-minute-delayed quote, plus a snapshot of the stock, including price and volume, market capitalization, dividend information, valuation, and other ratios, etc. A small 30-day chart for the stock is also shown.

On the left are links for an extensive collection of other data, including a full quote, charts, company summary, financials, etc. from a variety of partners. Data is supplied by Market Guide, Iverson Financial, Vickers Stock Research, Reuters, PRNewswire, Businesswire, and other sources.

You can also track your own portfolio using Northern Light's Portfolio option.

Search News

This interface provides searching of 2 weeks of articles from 70 sources, U.S. and international, including 33 news wires (such as

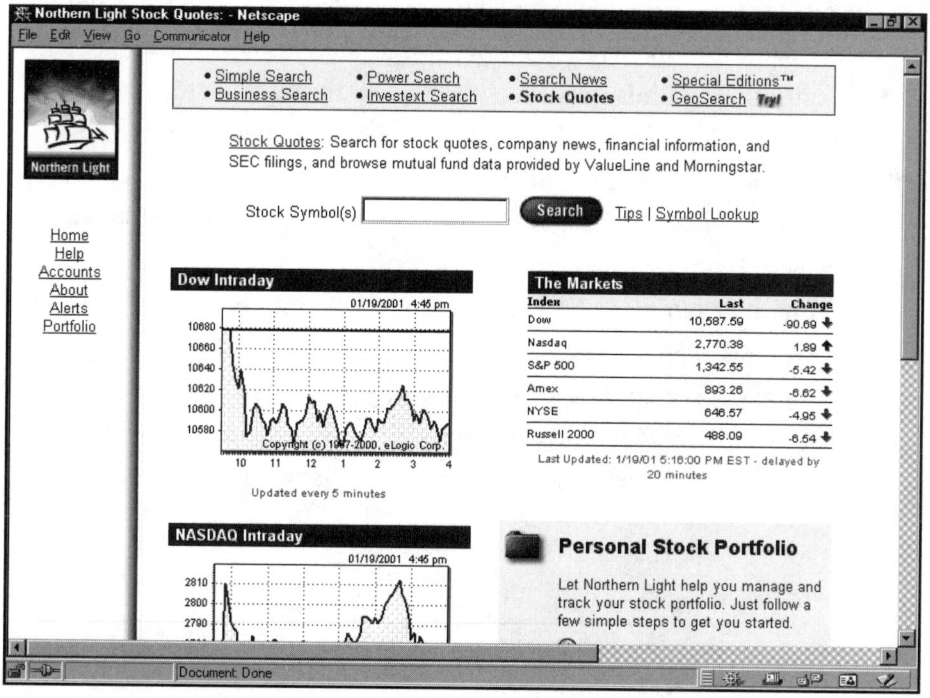

Figure 9.6 Northern Light's Stock Quotes Search page

AP News, UPI, and PR Newswire). These articles are free (earlier articles from theses sources are available on a pay-per-view basis by using the Power Search form). The search page also shows a few headlines with links to additional headlines, plus links to weather for the world's major cities and sports scores and schedules for U.S. professional teams. Search features such as Boolean, which are available in other sections of Northern Light, are also usable here.

You can specify the following:

- Subject, using the main query box
- Time frame (Last Two Hours, Today's News, Last Two Weeks)
- News category (business, computing, press releases, politics, etc.)
- Sorting results by relevance for date and time

Geo Search

This unique approach allows you to search the Northern Light database and specify the geographic origin (if in the U.S. or Canada) associated with the page. It allows you to find businesses and other organizations within a distance that you designate. This feature utilizes technology from Vicinity Corp., which converts geographic indications found within the page to latitude and longitude. Search features such as Boolean, which are available in other sections of Northern Light, are also usable here.

A term or terms must be entered in the "Search for" box.

With this search form you can:

- Specify geographic location by
    Street address (must also specify city and state or province)
    City (must also specify state or province)
    State or province
    ZIP code
    Telephone area code
- Designate an approximate radius to be covered (1, 5, 10, 25, 50, or 100 miles)
- Search for either U.S. or Canadian sites

Results show the matching addresses associated with the page and provide a link that will generate a map (from MAPBLAST) with the location(s) indicated by an asterisk.

Proprietary Content (Special Collection)

In addition to searching the Web, a Northern Light search also covers over 7,000 "premium" sources, including magazines, journals, newsletters, news wires, books, newspapers, and pamphlets. In results pages, these are identified by the "Special Collection" notation on the top line of the record. Abstracts are shown for free and the full document can be purchased with a credit card. Northern Light also offers an Enterprise Account Service, which provides multiple subaccounts, direct billing, usage reports, and other features.

To see a list of the titles in the Special Collection, click the "Special Collection" link found in various places, or go to the Help screens and click on "Special Collection."

Alerts

Northern Light offers an easy-to-use alerting service that covers Web pages, proprietary material, and news. This e-mail-delivered service allows easy and free tracking of companies, people, issues, and other topics. When you click the "Create Alert" link, you have the choice of using the Simple, Power, Business, Investext, or News search forms, along with all of the usual Northern Light search options such as Boolean and truncation. The Create Alert form steps you through the setup and allows you to sample results. For any researcher who remembers paying several dollars a week for such an alert on a single publication, these types of alerting features on Northern Light and elsewhere are hard to believe, but indeed true. Take advantage of them!

You'll also notice a small "Save this Search as an Alert" link on most results pages that allows you to easily convert your current search into an Alert.

"Special Editions"

Northern Light provides a small, but frequently added-to, collection of topic-specific pages, each containing selected links on subjects of current interest (e.g., Banking Industry, Managed Care, Autism) compiled by Northern Light's team of librarians and information specialists. These provide a good starting point for anyone interested in those particular issues.

SUMMARY OF NORTHERN LIGHT

Northern Light, with one of the largest of the Web search engine databases, has two major unique features: (1) integrated searching of its Special Collection of over 7,000 proprietary publications, and (2) automatic classification of pages. Northern Light's automatic classification is used to organize results into Custom Search Folders and also to create a very large, browsable, and searchable hierarchical Web directory.

With its focus on research, its large database, its proprietary collection, its wide array of search options, and its automatic classification, Northern Light is a first choice for many serious searchers. For any exhaustive searches, you'll want to put Northern Light on your list of engines to use. For terms that cross several fields—and when you'd like that aspect sorted out for you—be sure to use Northern Light. The presence of Northern Light's proprietary collection means that it's not just a Web search engine, but a large bibliographic database and document delivery service. For many users, it also serves as a reminder that not all research sources are Web resources—that there is a tremendous store of "traditional" journal and other literature that should not be ignored.

CHAPTER 10

Yahoo!
www.yahoo.com

OVERVIEW

Yahoo!, one of the first "finding tools" on the Web, still remains a powerful search engine, particularly because it integrates its primary nature as a directory with indexing and some useful searching features such as truncation, Boolean (minimal), and phrase searching. Yahoo! has three primary strengths: (1) It effectively integrates searching, directory functions, and other resources (such as news and a larger Web database); (2) it has a strong collection of portal and personalization features; and (3) it continues its entrenched position as the best-known tool among the general populace. With the Yahoo! directory now substantially smaller than its major directory competitor, Open Directory, Yahoo!'s effective integration of

Strengths 	Weaknesses 
• Extensive classified collection closely integrated into searching • Truncation • Automatic link to Google • Retrieving words are highlighted • Large selection of non-U.S. versions	• Minimal Boolean and field searching • Yahoo! database itself is very small

resources is probably the most important reason for serious searchers to continue paying close attention to it.

The number of sites in Yahoo!'s directory database is somewhere around 1 million records, but with its linkage to the Google database, it effectively provides access to 1 billion pages.

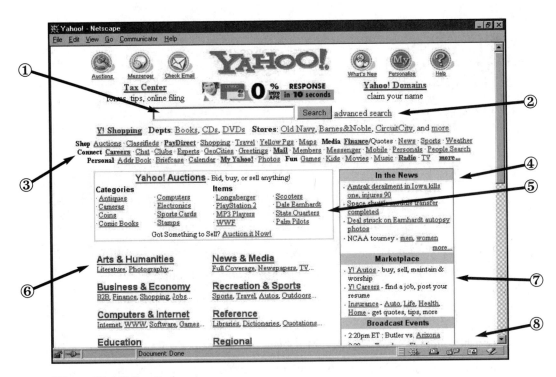

Figure 10.1 Yahoo!'s home page

YAHOO!'S HOME PAGE

① **Search box** (enter words, simplified Boolean query, or phrases)

② **"Advanced Search" link**

③ **Links to:**

- **Yahoo! Shopping and Auction sites**
- **Yahoo! Media sites** (News, Sports, Stock Quotes, TV, and Weather pages)
- **Yahoo! Personal options**—My Yahoo!, Address Book, Calendar, etc.

> • **Yahoo! Connect, Fun, etc.**—Click on "More" for a clearly presented site map.

④ **News Headlines**

⑤ **Yahoo!'s Shopping/Auctions Directory**

⑥ **The top-level Yahoo! directory classification**

⑦ **Yahoo! site promotions**

⑧ **Beneath the area shown:**

> • "Local Yahoo!s" for 23 **countries** and U.S. **cities** and states
>
> • Yahoo! **Channels:** "More Yahoo!s"

WHAT HAPPENS BEHIND THE SCENES

Yahoo! searches through five areas of its databases when a query is submitted:

- Yahoo! Categories
- Yahoo! Web Sites
- Web "pages"—the Google database
- News Articles
- Yahoo!'s Net Events—Webcasts, online discussions with personalities, chat rooms

Categories and Web sites will be displayed automatically (unless the list of categories alone fills the page). To get to the Google (non-directory) listings, news, and Net events, you need to click the appropriate link on a results page.

If a string of terms is entered with no qualifiers, Yahoo! ANDs them together. Those results are sorted by relevancy based on:

- How many of the query words were matched
- Field (title weighs higher than URL or body text)
- Level of the Yahoo! category matched—When the word searched is a word in a Yahoo! category, the higher-level category matches rank higher than deeper-level categories.

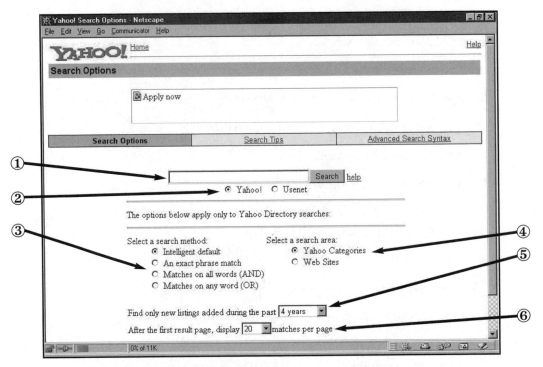

Figure 10.2 Yahoo!'s Advanced Search page

YAHOO!'S ADVANCED SEARCH PAGE

① Query box

② Choice of Yahoo! or Usenet (deja.com)

③ Choice of relevance ranking, phrase, AND, OR, or name

④ Choice of Yahoo! Categories or Web sites

⑤ Choice of date range (1 day to 4 years)

⑥ Choice of display (10, 20, 50, or 100 results per page)

Yahoo!'s Advanced Search page is actually more of a "settings" page than an advanced search page. With it you can:

- Change the default from Yahoo!'s standard relevance ranking ("Intelligent default" with terms ANDed) to an OR or an AND

- Have it default to returning Web sites first instead of categories

- Choose a time frame of from 1 day to 4 years

- Specify that 10, 20, 50, or 100 results be displayed

The Usenet radio button under the query box will take your search into Google's Usenet interface.

SEARCH FEATURES

Boolean Logic

+word To AND a term, use a plus sign directly in front of the word.

-word To NOT a term, use a minus sign directly in front of the word.

Field Searching

Only two fields are searchable in Yahoo!: title and URL. Each are searched using a one-letter prefix with a colon or the more standard prefixes for these two fields.

Title

t: or title:

Examples: t:mozart   title:mozart

t:"Czech Republic"   title:"Czech Republic"

URL

u: or url:

Example: u:intel   url:intel

Phrase Searching

For phrases, use double quotes: " "

Example: "World War II"

On the Search Options page you can also specify phrase searching as a setting, but it's much easier just to use the quotation marks on the home page.

Truncation

*Use an asterisk to truncate words.

Example: manufact*

Yahoo! also performs automatic truncation, for example the query "Belarus" also retrieves "Belarussian."

Conveniently, Yahoo! highlights the words responsible for retrieving the record.

Case-Sensitivity

Yahoo! is not case-sensitive and cannot distinguish between "White" and "white."

Order of Syntax

If you mix the Boolean and field search features in the same statement, the operators must be applied in the following order:

$$+ \quad - \quad title: \quad url:$$

RESULTS PAGES

When utilizing Yahoo!'s query box (vs. browsing the categories), Yahoo! will first display a list of Yahoo! categories that match your query, followed by specific sites from Yahoo!'s own database of selected, categorized sites (see Figure 10.3). If there are no matches for sites, the search will automatically be carried over into the Google database, and those results will be displayed. Keep in mind that the Google results are neither selective nor categorized.

Yahoo! provides one standard output format. Records are listed in relevance-ranked order. On the options page there is a choice of 10, 20, 50, or 100 records to be displayed per page.

At the top of results pages is a navigation bar leading to the matching categories, Web sites, Web pages (from Google), Related News, and Net Events.

By clicking on any of the search engine links shown at the bottom of a Yahoo! results page, the search is automatically carried into that engine. (But once there you may need to modify your search for compatibility of syntax.)

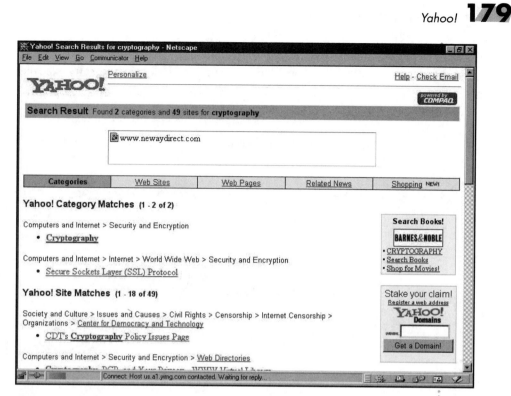

Figure 10.3 Yahoo!'s results page

YAHOO!'S DIRECTORY

For the serious searcher, Yahoo!'s classification of sites is its greatest strength, particularly the degree to which it integrates searching with browsing.

When "browsing" through categories, Yahoo! provides a line showing where you are in the hierarchy, and you can click on any part of that line to go back to that level. Beneath that you will see further subcategories, followed by those sites classified at the current level (see Figure 10.4).

Beside the query box on category pages is an option to search either all of Yahoo! or just within the current category. Take advantage of this to separate out unwanted aspects of a term. If you're looking for virus in connection with disease, go into the Health category and then search within that category. That will eliminate the occurrences of *computer virus* in your results.

The "@" sign next to a category means that it's cross-referenced from another category. Within categories, look especially for the "Web Directories" subcategory. This is where Yahoo! lists *metasites*, those small, specialized collections of links that can be invaluable for getting to know the major Web resources for a particular subject.

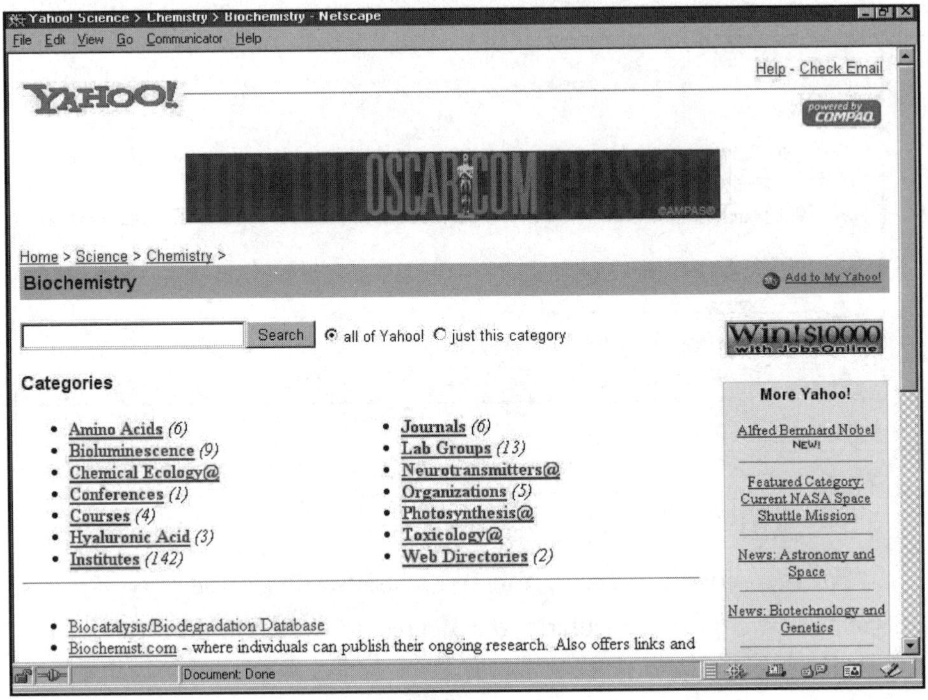

Figure 10.4 Page resulting from clicking on Science, then Chemistry, then Biochemistry

PORTAL AND PERSONALIZATION FEATURES

Personalization

Yahoo! has a personalized page (My Yahoo!) to rival any of the other portal sites. To get to the personal page, look for the small "Personalize" or "My Yahoo!" link on the home page. With My Yahoo! you can specify which categories of news you would like to see, set up a detailed personal portfolio, view the weather, and further make the page fit your own interests. Perhaps most importantly, with Yahoo!'s News Clipper service you can set up your own current awareness searches.

Portal Features

Yahoo! provides one of the largest collections of portal features. They're found under the collection of links labeled "Shopping," "Media," "Connect," and "Personals" near the top of the home page and at the bottom of the home page under "More Yahoo!s." The latter collection is organized as "channels" with a collection of topic-specific tools under each category. Many of the features in "More Yahoo!s" are also found in the first collection of links.

Among the features shown under the listings near the top of the pages are:

- **Shop**: Auctions, Classifieds, Shopping, Travel, Yellow Pages, Maps
- **Media**: News, Sports, Stock Quotes, TV, Weather
- **Connect**: Chat, Clubs, Games, GeoCities (free home pages), Greetings, Invites (to create and manage invitations to events), Free E-mail, Messenger, Personals, People Search (white pages), For Kids
- **Personal**: My Yahoo!, Address Book, Calendar, Briefcase (for accessing selected files remotely), Photos, Alerts, Bookmarks, Companion (to personalize your browser), Bill Pay

The "more" link at the end of the collection leads to a very nice listing of these features with a short explanation of what they mean.

The channels listed under "More Yahoo!s" at the bottom of the page are organized under eight headings:

- **Guides**: Autos, Careers, Health, Outdoors, Pets, Real Estate, Yahooligans!
- **Entertainment**: Top, Astrology, Broadcast, Games, Movies, Music, Net Events, Television

- **Finance**: Top, Banking, Bill Pay, Insurance, Loans, Taxes, Finance Vision
- **Local**: Top, Classifieds, Events, Lodging, Maps, Restaurants, Yellow Pages
- **News**: Top Stories, Business, Entertainment, Lottery, Politics, Sports, Technology, Weather
- **Publishing**: Briefcase, Clubs, Invites, Photos, Home Pages, Message Boards, Store
- **Small Business**: Top, Business Marketplace, Web Site Hosting, Store Building
- **Access Yahoo! Via**: For using Yahoo! on wireless devices

OTHER FEATURES

Transfer of Your Search to Other Engines

A unique feature of Yahoo! is the automatic transfer of a search into a variety of other engines. This makes Yahoo! a good starting place for searches where it will be useful to look at a smaller number of more-select pages first and then go on to the larger engines. Look at the bottom of results pages for links to other search engines. By clicking on these, the query will be transferred automatically without your having to retype it. Once at the other search engine's site, however, you may want to check the syntax to make sure it is compatible.

Local Yahoo!s

These are Yahoo!'s country-specific and U.S. city-specific versions. They're specific not just in terms of a native-language interface, but also in terms of specialized content for the locality. Among Web directories, no other has this level of international/localized coverage. The countries or regions covered are Denmark, France, Germany, India, Italy, Norway, Spain, Sweden, U.K. & Ireland, Asia, Australia

& New Zealand, China, Chinese, Hong Kong, Japan, Korea, Singapore, Taiwan, Argentina, Brazil, Canada, Mexico, and Spain.

SUMMARY OF YAHOO!

Yahoo! is a Web directory more than a search engine. Its own database is small (compared to the large search engines), but everything in it is categorized and selective. Through its partnership with Google, however, it also effectively searches perhaps the largest general Web collection. As the best-known general-purpose Web directory, it should be considered whenever browsing—as opposed to searching—is the aim. It can also be used to avoid having to look at a large number of sites when only a small set of search answers are needed. Since pages must meet Yahoo!'s editorial criteria to be entered into the database, the quality of sites tends to be higher than you may find, on average, in a large search engine. The searcher can also easily take advantage of Yahoo!'s integration of news and other resources as well as Yahoo!'s large collection of portal features. The serious searcher may want to take a look at "My Yahoo!," particularly for its News Clipper service (which provides personalized current-awareness searches).

CHAPTER 11

Meta-Search Tools

With eight or more major search engines available, wouldn't it be wonderful to have a means to search a number of them at once? Great idea! The good news is that it's possible and there are dozens of sites that allow you to search multiple engines simultaneously. The bad news is that the results often fall short of what you might expect.

There are basically two approaches to addressing the multi-engine-search problem. One is "meta-search sites," which are available free on the Web. The other is by use of a "client" meta-search program—that is, a program resident on your computer that aids in the searching of multiple engines. The meta-search sites are free and easy-to-use, but have major drawbacks in terms of the completeness with which they do the job. The "client-side" programs do a much more complete job, but involve the downloading (perhaps purchasing) of a program and several more steps to get to your results. We'll look at just a sampling from each of the two categories here.

META-SEARCH SITES

These free Web sites have the main advantage of ease of use, without the necessity of downloading any software, but there are important drawbacks.

The drawbacks are most evident by use of an example. In the chart below, a search was done on the word "Hilgreave" in several search engines, then in some of the more popular meta-search engines. If you spend a few moments examining the chart, you'll probably be able to make two or three significant conclusions (or at least observations), which may bring home the major considerations to keep in mind when using these tools. (If your favorite meta-search engine is not shown, try the same search in it.)

Table 11.1 Example of Meta-Search Engine Coverage						
	Done Directly	**via Dogpile**	**via ixquick**	**via MetaCrawler**	**via ProFusion**	**via Search.com**
AltaVista	41	41	10	10	19	10
Excite	17		12	10		5
HotBot	18		12			
Lycos	183 (1)	183			10	12
Google	18			11		
Northern Light	27					
Fast Search	44		13			
TOTAL	-	290	62	28	37	14

(1) Lycos included many discussion group postings

In particular, if there are more than a handful of relevant sites to be found in the Web search engines, the meta-search engines often miss most of them. This is caused by a number of factors, including limits imposed by the service on the number of records retrieved from individual engines, time-outs where the meta-search service simply cuts off the search within an engine if it takes too long, failure to adequately translate the query into the specific syntax required by the target engine, and other factors. Fortunately, some meta-search engines do return all of the records that are really there (but have other drawbacks).

The three major weaknesses of meta-search engines are that (1) they often strictly limit the number of records they'll retrieve from any single engine (sometimes to as few as 10); (2) they often will not transfer even slightly sophisticated queries to the engines; and (3) in most cases, they don't search more than two or three of the five largest search engines.

Creating one of these sites is not difficult, which helps account for their large number. Yahoo!'s category for these engines lists over 100 of them. Some are basically a collection of search boxes that have been copied and pasted from the various search engines. Some go considerably further than that and do address at least one or two of the problems just mentioned.

For the most part, the meta-search engines differ from one another in the following ways:

- The specific search engines they cover
- The number of search engines that can be searched at a time
- Their ability to transfer more-sophisticated queries—such as those including phrases, Boolean statements, etc.—to the "target" search engines
- Their limits on how many records they retrieve from each engine (which can be as low as 10)
- The length of time they're willing to spend searching each engine (before they time-out)
- How output is presented, including whether or not they eliminate duplicate hits from the various engines

The meta-search engines are most useful and effective when you're looking for something very obscure, if for your particular search you think that there exist fewer than 10 sites of interest (or you don't care to identify more than 10 sites), and if your search only involves a single word or phrase. There are many records that are found in some of the smaller engines that are not retrieved by any of the three or four largest engines, and it can be time-consuming to individually search all of the major engines. The meta-search engines do indeed allow you to very quickly scan many engines for that obscure term or phrase.

It's not feasible to cover all 100-plus of these meta-search engines here. Instead, we'll look at five of the more popular and representative ones. These five were chosen because, between them, they aptly demonstrate a good sampling of the variety of capabilities and approaches taken:

- Dogpile—www.dogpile.com
- ixquick—ixquick.com
- MetaCrawler—www.metacrawler.com
- ProFusion—www.profusion.com.
- Search.com—search.com

For an extensive list of meta-search sites, in Yahoo! go to: Computers and Internet > Internet > World Wide Web > Searching the Web > Search Engines and Directories > All-in-One Search Pages

For each of the following brief profiles, a summary is shown to highlight several of the more critical factors to examine when considering the effectiveness of these tools. "Major engines covered" refers to how many of the nine engines with over 200 million records are searched by the meta-search engine. "Total engines/directories searched" refers to the total number of general search engines or general Web directories searched (some of which may be very small). "Boolean option" refers to whether the user can at least effectively use ANDs and ORs or their equivalent. (Remember not to expect any syntax more sophisticated than Boolean in any of the meta-search engines.) "Maximum records per engine" refers to the retrieval limits imposed by the meta-search engine.

DOGPILE
www.dogpile.com

Major engines searched:	3
Total engines/directories searched:	12
Boolean option:	Yes
Duplicates removed or combined:	No
Maximum records per engine:	Unlimited
Maximum records	Unlimited

Dogpile is a meta-search engine that identifies and retrieves as many (of the same) records from the target engines as are retrieved when those engines are searched individually. Dogpile makes a stab at translating queries into the nearest similar syntax for each of the target engines. This works well sometimes but not others.

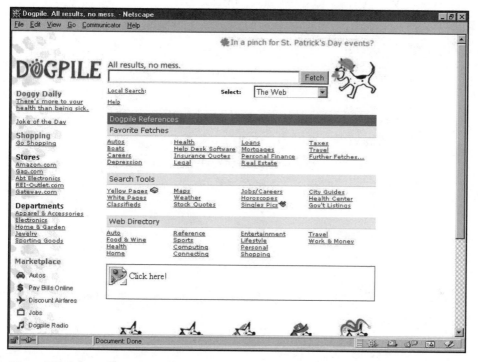

Figure 11.1 Dogpile's home page

Dogpile allows a choice of searching the Web, Usenet, FTP, news, auctions, images, SmallBiz (Hypermart), and audio/MP3.

By clicking Custom Search, you can specify the order in which queries are sent to the various engines. Engines may also be deleted from the list of those to be searched.

The "Local Search" link on the Dogpile home page allows you to narrow your search to a specific geographic region by entering a U.S. city and state or ZIP code. Dogpile also provides a directory and a collection of other services and links.

Dogpile Searches These Services:

- Web Search Engines and Directories:

• Yahoo!	• GoTo.com	• Lycos
• Go.com	• AltaVista	• Google
• Direct Hit	• LookSmart	• Open Directory
• Sprinks	• RealNames	• Dogpile Directory

- Usenet:

• AltaVista	• Usenet
• Deja.com	• Deja.com's archival database
• FTP:	• Fast FTP Search

- News:
  - Thunderstone
- Auctions: GoTo.com
- Audio/MP3:

• Astraweb	• AudioGalaxy	• Gigabeat
• MP3Board		

- Images: Ditto.com
- SmallBiz: Hypermart
- A variety of other sources (yellow pages, white pages, maps, etc.) are provided by the collection of links on Dogpile's home page. They are not covered by a regular Dogpile search.

Search Syntax

Dogpile attempts to translate any syntax the user inputs into syntax appropriate to the target search engine. It often does so very well, but not always. In AltaVista, in a search using pluses and minuses, it turned the minus into a NOT and searched it in AltaVista's Main Search (where the minus would have been an appropriate choice).

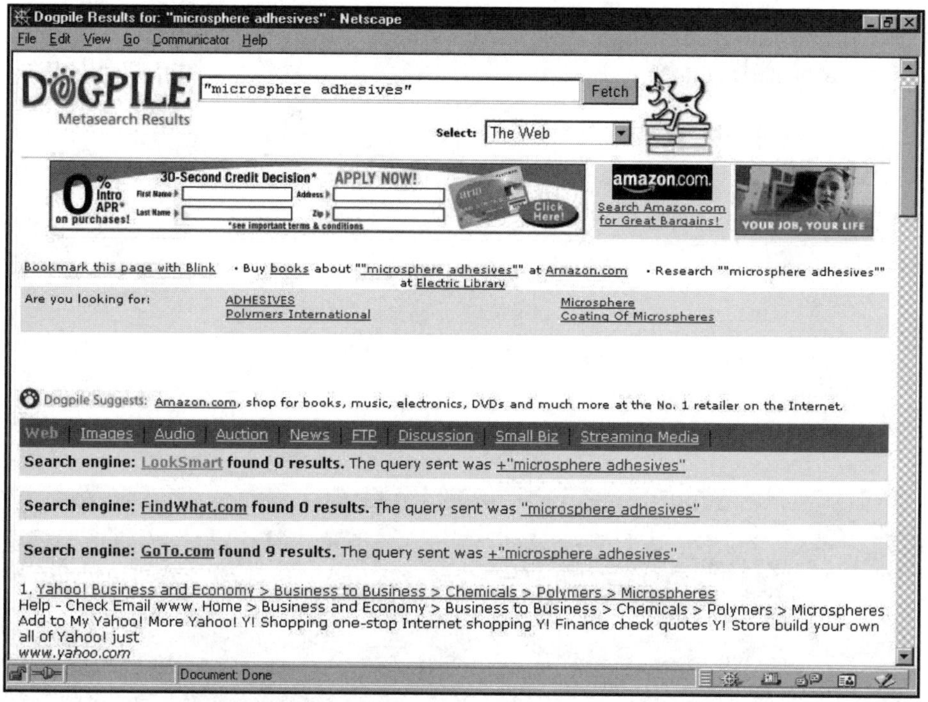

Figure 11.2 Dogpile's results page

Waiting Time Permitted

Dogpile does not impose a maximum waiting time.

Limits on Number of Records

Dogpile imposes no limits on the number of records retrieved.

Arrangement of Output

Output is arranged by search engine. Dogpile displays results from three search engines at a time, unless those produce fewer than 10 records, in which case more than three search engines will be shown. Up to 10 records per search engine are displayed and additional records are viewed by clicking the "Next set from…" link, which will take you directly to results pages from that search engine. The "Next Set of Search Engines" link is used to go to see results from the next three (or more) search engines.

IXQUICK
ixquick.com

Major engines searched:	4
Total engines/directories searched:	14
Boolean option:	Yes
Duplicates removed or combined:	Yes
Maximum records per engine:	10
Maximum records:	<100

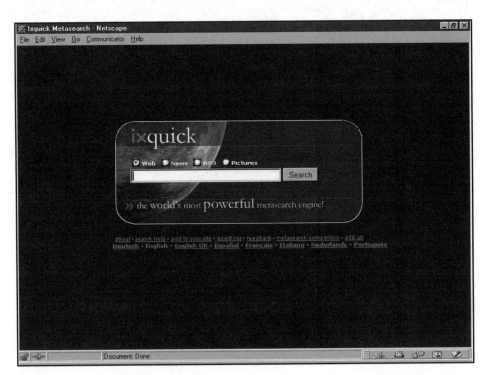

Figure 11.3 ixquick's home page

ixquick searches several major engines and ranks results primarily based upon how many engines listed the site in the top ten. ixquick covers more of the major engines than most meta-search sites, and though it only lists a few sites from each engine it allows easy access to other records found in the individual engines. It also eliminates duplicates and allows use of most typical search features (Boolean, truncation, case-sensitivity, etc.). As well as Web sites, ixquick also allows searching of news, MP3, and image sources.

Engines/Directories Searched:

- AltaVista
- AOL
- Euroseek
- Excite
- Fast Search

- GoTo
- HotBot
- Infoseek
- LookSmart
- MSNt

- NBCi
- Webcrawler
- XRefer
- Yahoo!

ixquick also allows searching of seven **news** sources, five **MP3** sources, and eight **image** sources. For each of those categories, check boxes allow you to choose the specific sources to be searched.

Search Syntax

ixquick accepts virtually any syntax (Boolean, truncation, and even field prefixes such as *title:*). However, it only sends these more sophisticated queries to the engines that handle the specific syntax. If you enter *title:passau*, you will only get back records from engines that use the *title:* syntax.

Waiting Time Permitted

ixquick does not allow the user to specify a waiting time, and it does not specify any particular time-out automatically set by the system.

Limits on Number of Records

The total is limited to somewhat less than 100 records, and usually less than 80.

Arrangement of Output

ixquick ranks results primarily based on how many engines listed the site in the top ten, then by the relative ranking of those sites within the engines. Additional records from each engine are reachable by means of a link to the engine included in records.

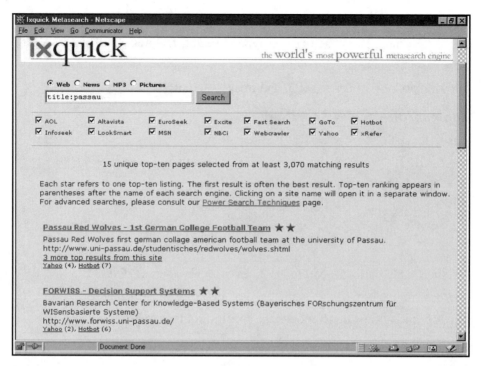

Figure 11.4 ixquick's results page

METACRAWLER

www.metacrawler.com

Major engines searched:	4
Total engines/directories searched:	14
Boolean option:	Yes
Duplicates removed or combined:	Yes
Maximum records per engine:	30
Maximum records	<300

MetaCrawler was one of the first meta-search sites and currently searches 14 search engines and Web directories. Two versions, Home Page and Power Search, are available. The latter provides additional functionality, with domain searching (continent, .edu, .com, .gov, etc.) and the ability to specify time-out; number of

Figure 11.5 MetaCrawler's home page

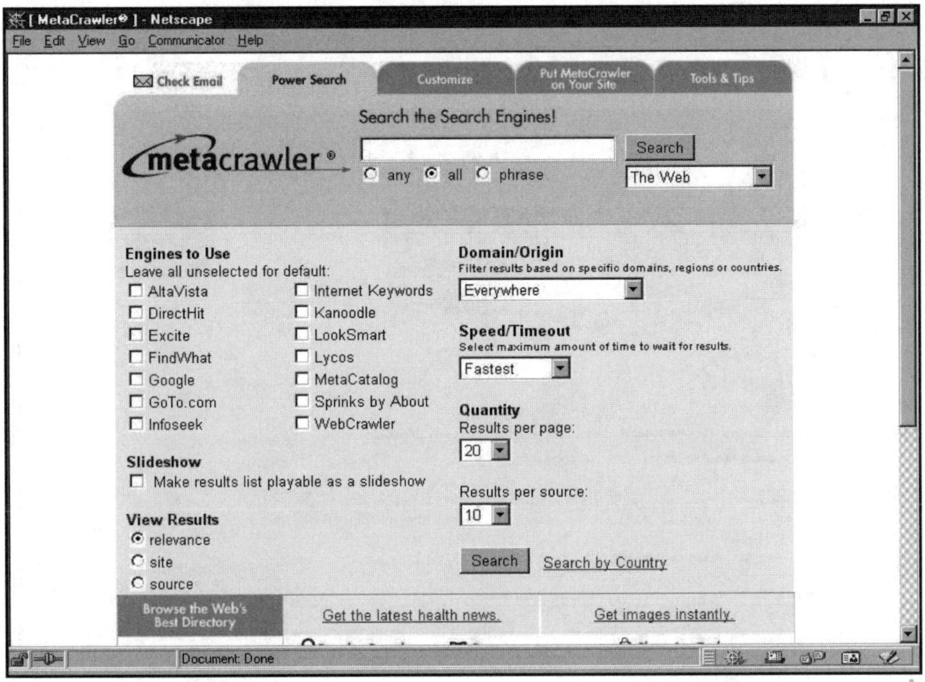

Figure 11.6 MetaCrawler's Power Search page

results per page; number of results per source (10, 20, or 30); output by relevance, site, or source; and selection of engines/directories. Both versions provide limited Boolean capabilities by allowing the choice of "any" or "all" words, or phrase searching. Search preferences can be set by using the Customize tab. MetaCrawler also provides access to the LookSmart directory and a variety of other resources.

Engines/Directories Searched:

- AltaVista
- Direct Hit
- Excite
- FindWhat
- Google
- GoTo
- LookSmart

- Lycos
- RealNames
- Sprinks
- Thunderstone
- Webcrawler
- Yahoo!

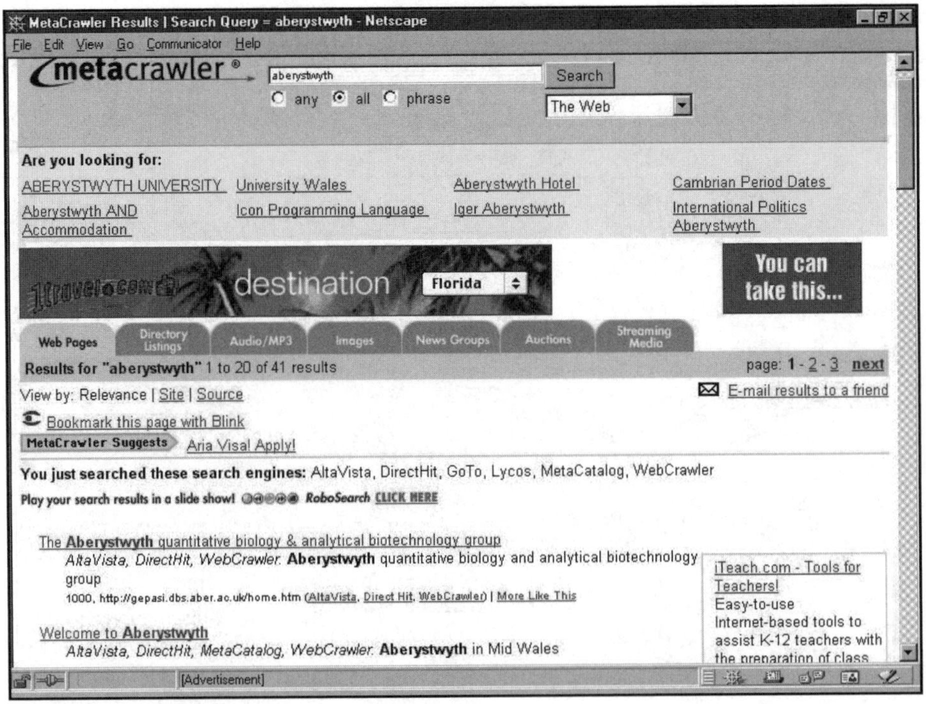

Figure 11.7 MetaCrawler's results page

Search Syntax

The searcher can specify that "any," "all," or "phrase" be applied to the words in the query. This is translated to the appropriate syntax for each of the engines.

Waiting Time Permitted

In Power Search, a time-out of up to 2 minutes can be specified.

Limits on Number of Records

With MetaCrawler's home page version, up to 10 records per engine can be retrieved. In Power Search mode, the user can specify 10, 20, or 30 records per source.

Arrangement of Output

Output is arranged by relevance ranking, by site (e.g., U.S. commercial sites), or source. MetaCrawler determines relevance by combining and normalizing the scores given by the various engines and expressing the resultant score as a number between 1 and 1,000. In the case of duplicates, MetaCrawler will list the site only once, but it will show which engines found the site and the detail provided by each engine. MetaCrawler also suggests related searches.

PROFUSION

www.profusion.com

Major engines searched:	3
Total engines/directories searched:	9
Boolean option:	Yes
Duplicates removed or combined:	Yes
Maximum records per engine:	approx. 20
Maximum records	<200

ProFusion has one of the more sophisticated interfaces and allows fairly extensive user control over results. It also allows a full Boolean statement to be used (and carried over into those engines that can accept it). However, as with most meta-search engines,

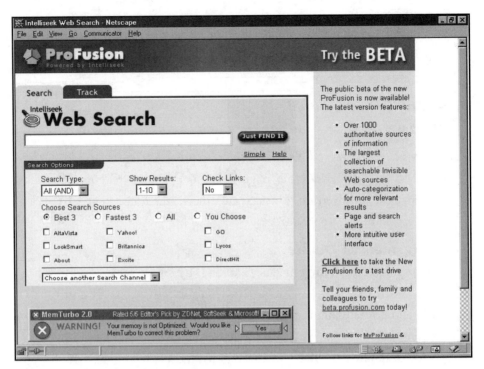

Figure 11.8 ProFusion's home page

some of this sophistication is wasted because of the fact that ProFusion imposes small maximums (10 to 25) on the number of records it will retrieve from each engine. ProFusion also provides the option of checking links to see if they're active. ProFusion is in the process of introducing an enhanced version, but will maintain its "classic" interface as well.

Engines/Directories Searched:

- About.com
- AltaVista
- Direct Hit
- Excite

- LookSmart
- Lycos
- Yahoo!

Of these, you can choose to search:

- The "Best 3"
- The "Fastest 3"
- All

You can also select "You choose" and pick the engines you wish to search.

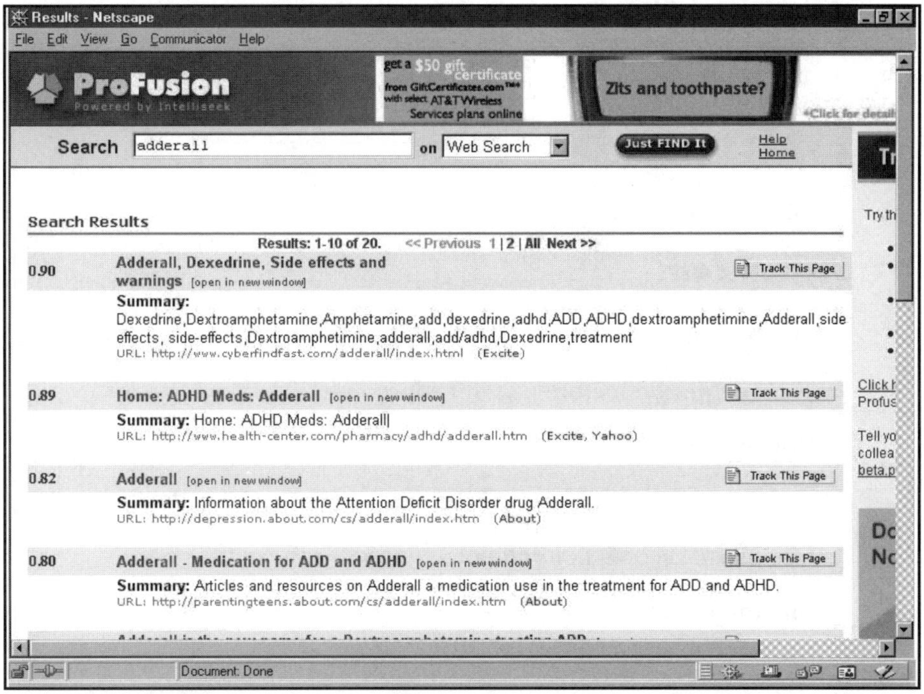

Meta-Search Tools

Figure 11.9 ProFusion's results page

Search Syntax

From the Search Type box, you can select Simple, All, Any, Boolean, or Phrase. Profusion supports full Boolean (AND, OR, NOT) plus NEAR. For the engines that have Boolean, but not NEAR (Excite and WebCrawler), ProFusion changes a NEAR to an AND. This feature allows very useful control over the search and lets the user know what's taking place. If you wish to use Boolean queries, you must choose "Boolean" in the "Search mode" box.

Waiting Time Permitted

ProFusion does not provide a waiting-time option, nor does it specify what time limit may be set automatically by the system.

Limits on Number of Records

You can choose total output to be limited to 10, 20, 50, 99, or All records. "All" seems to translate into somewhat less than 200 records in any search.

Arrangement of Output

ProFusion eliminates duplicates, shows which engines contained each record, and lists them according to a relevance-ranking score.

SEARCH.COM (formerly SavvySearch)

search.com

Major engines searched:	3
Total engines/directories searched:	16
Boolean option:	Yes
Duplicates removed or combined:	Yes
Maximum records per engine:	10 or all
Maximum records	<50 or All

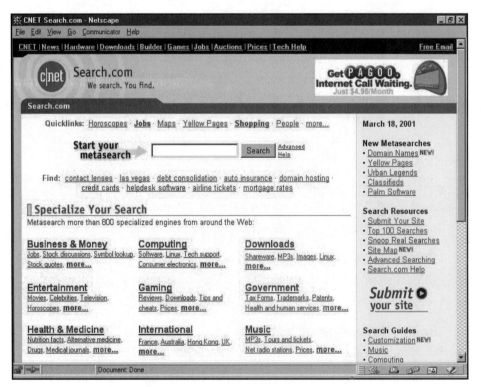

Figure 11.10 Search.com's home page

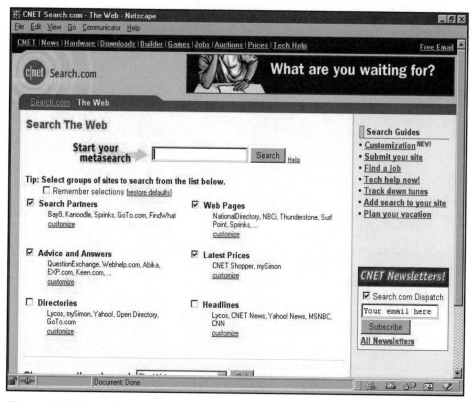

Figure 11.11 Search.com's Advanced Search page

Search.com, from CNET, provides a gateway to a collection of over 800 search engines, directories, online stores, Usenet archives, news archives, software libraries, etc. Many of these are very small collections or individual reference tools. Access to the full collection is provided through a directory on the Search.com home page. The main query box on the home page searches the search engines, directories, and "latest prices"—not the full collection. The Advanced link on the home page takes you to a page that allows you to pick the category of information to be searched (Web pages, directories, shopping, news, etc.). It also allows you to customize your search in each category by selecting, for example, which of the search engines should be included in the search.

Engines/Directories Searched:

Search.com offers the option of searching the following general search tools (plus over 700 more specialized sources):

- About.com
- AltaVista
- Britannica.com
- Clearinghouse (Argus)
- Direct Hit
- Galaxy
- GoTo.com
- HotBot
- LookSmart
- Lycos
- National Directory
- NBCi
- Open Directory
- RealNames
- Thunderstone
- Yahoo!

Search Syntax

Queries are transmitted to the target engines just as entered by the user. Therefore, if the searcher enters a Boolean query and a target engine cannot handle it, results will not necessarily be what was requested.

Waiting Time Allowed

Search.com doesn't provide a waiting-time option, nor does it specify what time limit may be set automatically by the system.

Limits on Number of Records Displayed

In the default "sort by relevance," Search.com will typically display fewer than 50 records. It will search the "fastest" engines and give you the option of searching all of the search engines and directories (typically returning fewer than 100). The first few records from a search engine will be shown, and there will be a link that will take you directly to the search engine's results page, thereby making all records from that engine available.

Arrangement of Output

Records are displayed by relevance (as measured by how many engines retrieved the record and the order in which they appeared in those engines).

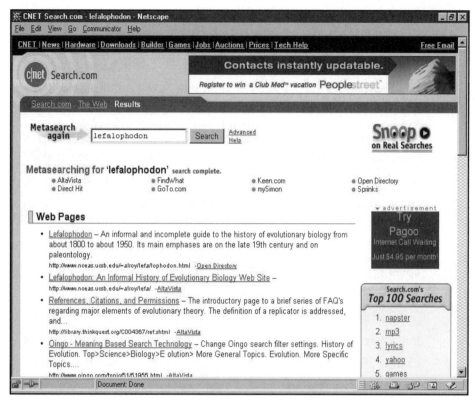

Figure 11.12 Search.com's results page

OTHER META-SEARCH SITES

We can look forward to new meta-search engines popping up fairly frequently, often using unique and creative approaches. The popularity of particular meta-search engines seems to run in waves. You'll hear mention of one several times in a row, then another takes its place. Try some of them out, see which engines they cover, see if they deliver results in ways you like. Most importantly, be aware of what they are not covering. If you want to explore, choose a few from the Yahoo! category mentioned earlier.

"CLIENT" META-SEARCH PROGRAMS

For multi-engine searching, the alternative to the meta-search sites is utilization of a "client" meta-search program. This is a program on your computer that serves as an "intelligent agent" to do the work that you would otherwise do in dealing with several engines.

The idea of using these "intelligent agents," which can go several steps beyond the meta-search engines that have been discussed here, has been extensively explored, and several such programs have been developed and refined. Most notable among these at the moment are Copernic and BullsEye, which, by means of a program downloaded to the user's computer, search a variety of Web search engines, sort out the results, allow further local searching, and perform a variety of related tasks.

These programs, to varying degrees, have the advantages of covering more engines than any of the current meta-search sites, allowing further manipulation of results, and allowing further processing after you've logged off the Internet. It can be argued that their greatest importance and utility lies in the management of data after it has been located by the search engines themselves. The main disadvantage is that they present one more step, often involving many more clicks, between the searcher and the product. If the "product" is the location of the required relevant sites, these tools may be largely superfluous for many skilled search engine users. If the "product" is an organized and manipulable collection of retrieved sites, these programs can be a powerful assistant. Since this latter side of searching is only on the periphery of the thrust of this book, we will take just a brief glimpse at what this software offers.

BullsEye

BullsEye, from Intelliseek, Inc., is available in a trial version. The standard version (BullsEye) and advanced version (BullsEye Pro) can be purchased. The standard version offers the following:

- Searching of over 800 sources (search engines, directories, databases, etc.)

- Specialized searches by category (Web, News, Shopping, Multimedia, Discussion, Jobs, Books, Software, Computers, Business, References, Health, Entertainment, Colleges, etc.)
- Boolean and proximity capabilities tailored to the target engine
- Filtering by country, site type, URL, size, date, etc.
- Elimination of duplicates and dead links
- Enhanced relevance ranking using Verity technology
- Off-line analysis and refinement of results
- Extensive report-generating capabilities
- Exporting of searches to other users
- Saved searches and search alerting
- Etc.

The trial version of BullsEye can be downloaded at www.intelliseek.com. The advanced version offers extensive search-tracking capabilities not available in the regular version.

Copernic

Copernic, from Copernic Technologies, Inc., is available in a free version (no expiration date) and two advanced versions that require a purchase. The free version offers the following:

- Searching of 80 sources
- Searching by seven categories (Web, Newsgroups, Email Addresses, Books, Hardware, Software, one user-selected language)
- Simple Boolean (AND, OR)
- Elimination of duplicates and dead links
- Choice of six languages (English, French, German, Italian, Portuguese, Spanish)
- Translation feature
- Search saving and tracking
- Etc.

Copernic can be downloaded at www.copernic.com. The non-free versions offer more sources, 55 specialty categories, and no ads.

SUMMARY OF META-SEARCH TOOLS

These tools are worth examination by the serious searcher. Choosing one or two and getting to know them in detail can enhance searching ease and speed, but they may or may not augment your searching "power." Each of these puts an additional layer between you and the search engine, and you'll definitely lose many benefits of the individual engines (especially field searching). The many added features and the increasingly valuable resources that are integrated into search engine results pages will be less accessible, if at all, when going through a meta-search tool. Whether and when to use these tools, in the end, comes down to a matter of the kind of searching you typically do, the kind of search you're doing at the moment, and how comfortable you've become with the tool and its features.

CHAPTER 12

Other Search Engines and Keeping Up

OTHER SEARCH ENGINES

The search engines that have been covered in this book are the larger, more powerful, and more popular ones. They're also services that have the intention of covering a significant portion of the Web without any limitation in terms of subject area or geographic origin. (Although it can be argued that U.S. Web sites are disproportionately indexed.) There are many other search engines available on the Web. Indeed, in the narrower, perhaps even more legitimate, sense of the term, any site that is "searchable" has a search engine. More to the point, though, is that there are a number of search engines that focus on Web sites from particular geographic areas—the U.K., for instance—or apply some other criteria to limit their coverage.

For an extensive list of these search engines, try the following category in Yahoo!:

> Computers and Internet > Internet > World Wide Web > Searching the Web > Search Engines and Directories

Another extensive list can be found on Danny Sullivan's Search Engine Watch site (discussed further below) in his Searchlinks section at searchenginewatch.com/links.

If you're looking for a search engine focusing on a particular country, also be sure to look at the country-specific versions of the search engines discussed in this book, particularly AltaVista, Excite, and Lycos, all of which have good international offerings.

KEEPING UP

The best way to keep up with changes in Web search engines is close observation. Periodically take a closer-than-usual look at the home pages, the advanced search pages, and the results pages. New features will usually be announced for several weeks on the home pages. Also look for links you haven't seen before and follow them. Unfortunately, you can't assume that the documentation will discuss the new features. Though the quality of documentation has improved greatly, the updating of documentation is still not always given high priority by some search engines.

Another way of keeping current is to take advantage of search engine news sites, journals, and conferences.

SEARCH ENGINE NEWS SITES

About.com Web Search

websearch.about.com

About.com covers a broad range of Web searching news, lists, links, and other features. Content includes not just general Web search engines but other search engines and tools for images, people, careers, chat, genealogy, etc. In addition, the site provides a Web Search Forum and a free e-mail newsletter. The About.com Web site named the first edition of this book as "Best Search Engine Book" for 1999.

Free Pint

freepint.co.uk

William Hann, a U.K.-based writer and Internet consultant, provides Free Pint, a free fortnightly e-mail newsletter focusing not specifically on Web search engines, but on Web research in general, with a lot of search engine content. Besides his own input, he draws on a variety of very qualified researchers from various fields for in-depth articles on using the Web for specific disciplines and applications. Though the content is universally useful, look here especially for good coverage of U.K. resources. As well as the newsletter, he hosts a forum (the "Bar") on Web research.

ResearchBuzz.com

researchbuzz.com

Tara Calishain, who produced the *Official Netscape Guide to Internet Research*, produces a very informative site and newsletter that, as she puts it, is designed to "cover the world of Internet research." Though that's a pretty big order, she makes a remarkably good stab at it and constantly uncovers valuable research-related tools, news, techniques, and just plain interesting facts not just for search engines but for the entire range of Web research sites. Her weekly e-mail newsletter is free.

Search Engine Showdown

searchengineshowdown.com

Greg Notess, widely published writer and speaker on Web searching, produces Search Engine Showdown, which provides both an overview of search engines and directories and also in-depth analysis of aspects such as size, overlap, inconsistencies, etc. Look to this site particularly for very perceptive analysis of these and other factors, as well as frequently updated statistics on size, overlap, dead links, and other variables. Greg also provides excellent coverage of news sources on the Web. A free monthly (or more frequent) newsletter is available, as is a search engine discussion group.

Search Engine Watch

searchenginewatch.com

Danny Sullivan, the leading journalist in the area of Web search engines, and Chris Sherman, co-author of *The Invisible Web*, maintain Search Engine Watch, a site that provides very up-to-date news and reports in a concise, readable style. The site provides an extremely valuable resource both for the Web site publisher and for the searcher. Look here for a wide range of information—technical and not-so-technical—about using search engines and about getting your own sites listed and appropriately ranked in search engines. Access to much of his site is free, but for some of the more in-depth material (particularly for Web site publishers) a subscription version is available. Search Engine Watch also provides a free monthly e-mail newsletter, and, for paying subscribers, a more detailed, twice-a-month newsletter.

The Extreme Searcher's Web Page

extremesearcher.com

This site is primarily for providing updates to this book. See page xxv for details on the purpose and content of the site.

CONFERENCES

Many organizations and associations sponsor conferences that contain a substantial amount of content related to Web searching. The following are conferences where "extreme searchers" are likely to congregate. For details on dates and locations, see the Web sites listed.

Internet Librarian, Internet Librarian International (London), InfoToday (formerly known as the National Online Meeting)

www.infotoday.com

Web Search University

www.onlineinc.com

Online Information (London)

www.online-information.co.uk

JOURNALS

For current articles relevant to making the most effective use of search engines, try the following:

EContent (formerly DATABASE)

Online, Inc.
213 Danbury Road
Wilton, CT 06897-4007
www.onlineinc.com

ONLINE

Online, Inc.
213 Danbury Road
Wilton, CT 06897-4007
www.onlineinc.com

Searcher: The Magazine for Database Professionals

Information Today, Inc.
143 Old Marlton Pike
Medford, NJ 08055
www.infotoday.com

The CyberSkeptic's Guide to Internet Research

Bibliodata
P.O. Box 61
Needham Heights, MA 02494
www.bibliodata.com

Information Today: The Newspaper for Users and Producers of Electronic Information Services

Information Today, Inc.
143 Old Marlton Pike
Medford, NJ 08055
www.infotoday.com

Conclusion

"So, c'mon, Ran. Tell us which one you really like best." The honest-to-goodness, cross-my-heart-hope-to-die, Eagle Scout's honor, answer is: "It depends." Of course, unless you skipped the rest of this book, you probably knew that answer already. More importantly, what might your own choice of "favorite" search engines depend upon?

If you are looking for a strong engine with a broad collection of added features, it might be AltaVista. If you want to cover not just the Web, but a wealth of journal and other literature, with strong, easy search capabilities, it might be Northern Light. If you are looking for broad retrieval, but prefer extreme simplicity, it might be Google or Fast Search. If you want a strong but user-friendly interface, it might be HotBot. If you want great portal features, it might be Excite or Lycos. If you primarily want the benefits of a directory, but would like to also cover a search-engine-size data-base, you might go for Yahoo!.

Beyond such generalizations, every search engine user has unique needs. It is probably a combination of features, and the factors of familiarity and comfort, that determine which search engine you typically go to first. Ask yourself what features you need (exhaustivity, image searching, date searching, etc.) and see which search engines provide that. Get intimately familiar with at least two search engines. On those engines, look in every nook and cranny.

Some very powerful and unique offerings are sometimes placed in less than obvious places on home pages and on results pages. The best method for finding these can be to lock your office door, go to the search engine, and "Click everywhere."

Not just with your favorites, but with all of the engines, keep a few facts in mind and the chances are good that the search engines will lead you to the information you need:

1. If you want to find everything on your topic, use more than one search engine.

2. If you want to locate the very best page on a subject, search more than one engine and look at the first 20 or so records.

3. Don't just use the home page version of an engine. The advanced or power search modes are often much better.

Occasionally pick two or three fairly precise searches of the type you frequently encounter and do some benchmarking. Look for the numbers retrieved and the relevance of the first 1-20 records retrieved. This will not only give you a feel for the differences, but will help keep you up-to-date in changes in sizes of databases, etc., and sometimes might even cause you to change your "favorites."

The more familiar you become with any search engine, the more readily you will recognize and assimilate any changes that take place. Be aware that many changes are "cosmetic," and for the marketing purpose of a "new look." The old familiar features are probably still there, but at a different location on the page and often with a name change. When you do notice multiple changes, chances are that at least one of them is not just cosmetic, but substantive. Explore those.

Remember that search engine services are still in their adolescence, maybe late adolescence, but adolescence, nonetheless. They are growing in stature and wisdom, but still have mild cases of acne and are very prone to fads and sometimes change for change's sake. This too will pass.

As with dealing with the human versions of adolescents, patience may be your most valuable attribute. Don't take minor weaknesses too seriously, and enjoy the positive changes. Look for and take advantages of the new and often impressive features.

As was said in the conclusion to the first edition of this book, search engines are providing us with amazing research capabilities. Stay tuned, it continues to get even better.

Search Engine-Related Terms

Author's Note: The following terms and phrases are defined in the context of Web search engines and may not be applicable in other contexts.

add-ons. Features and services attached to a search engine that are not directly a part of the searching function.

algorithm. A step-by-step procedure for solving a problem or achieving a task. In the context of search engines, the part of the service's program that performs a task such as identifying which pages should be retrieved or the ranking of pages that have been retrieved.

alternate text. In the HTML code for Web pages, the text that goes along with an image file and is to be displayed if, for some reason, the image does not display. In addition to that use, it can be useful for retrieval purposes for identifying and indexing the subject to which an image refers. Also, when using a browser, it's what pops up in the little yellow box when you hold your cursor over an image.

AND. The Boolean operator (or connector) that specifies the intersection of sets. When used between words in a search engine query, it specifies that only those records that contain both words are to be retrieved (the words preceding and following the AND). For example, "stomach AND growling" would only retrieve records containing both of those words. A plus sign immediately in front of a term can sometimes be substituted for the word "AND."

AOL. America Online, the most popular consumer online service.

applet. A small Java-based program used on a Web page to perform certain display, computational, or other functions. The term originates from the idea of "small applications programs."

bookmark. A feature found in Web browsers, analogous to bookmarks used in a book, that remembers the location of a particular Web page and adds it to a list so the page can be returned to easily. Netscape Navigator refers to these as "bookmarks,"while Microsoft Internet Explorer uses the term "favorites."

Boolean. Mathematical system of notation created by 19th century mathematician George Boole that symbolically represents a relationship between sets (entities). For information retrieval, it uses AND, OR, and NOT (or their equivalents) to identify those records that meet the criteria of having both of two terms within the record (AND), having either of two terms within the records (OR), or eliminating records that contain a particular term (NOT).

browser. Software that enables display of Web pages by interpreting HTML code, translating it, and performing related tasks. The first widely used browser was Mosaic, which evolved into Netscape. Internet Explorer is the browser developed by Microsoft.

case-sensitivity. The ability to recognize the difference between uppercase and lowercase. In information retrieval, it means the difference between possibly being able to recognize White as a name versus white as a color, or AIDS as the disease versus aids as something that provides assistance.

channels. Term used by some online services to organize their services, functions, and Web pages by subject area.

classification. Arrangement of Web sites by subject area, often using a hierarchical scheme with several levels of categories and subcategories.

co-occurrence. Occurrence of two or more specific terms within the same record. Analyzing the frequency of co-occurrence is one technique used to find records that are similar to a selected record.

concept-based retrieval. Retrieval based on finding records that contain words related to the concept searched for, not necessarily the specific word(s) searched for.

crawler. See "spider."

diacritical marks. Marks such as accents that are applied to a letter to indicate a different phonetic value.

directory (Web directory). Collection of Web page records classified by subject to enable easy browsing of the collection.

domain name. The part of a URL (Web address) that specifies the organization responsible for the Web page. Domain names always have at least two parts. The first part usually identifies the sponsoring organization (for instance, "microsoft"). The second part usually identifies the type of sponsor (for instance, ".com" for "commercial," "edu" for "educational," etc.).

favorites. See bookmarks.

field. A specific portion of a record, or Web page, such as title, metatags, URL, etc.

file extension. In a file name, such as letter.doc or house.gif, the part of the name that follows the period, usually indicating the type of file.

HTML (HyperText Markup Language). The coding language used to create Web pages, HTML tells a browser how to display a record, including specifications for such things as font, colors, location of images, identification of hypertext links, etc.

home page. The main page of a Web site. Also, the page designated by a user as the page that should be automatically brought up when the user's browser is loaded.

ISP. Internet Service Provider.

Java. A programming language designed for use on networks, particularly the Internet, which allows programs to be downloaded and run on a variety of platforms. JAVA is incorporated into Web pages with small applications programs called "applets" that provide features such as animation, calculators, games, etc.

JavaScript. A computer language used to write "scripts" for use in browsers to allow creation of such features as scrolling marquees, etc.

meta-search engines. Search services that search several individual search engines and then combine the results.

metatags. The portion (field) of the HTML coding for a Web page that allows the person creating the page to enter text describing the content of the page. The content of metatags is not shown on the page itself when the page is viewed in a browser window.

NEAR. A proximity connector that is used between two words to specify that a document (i.e., a Web page) should be retrieved only when those words are near one another in the document.

nesting. The use of parentheses to specify the way in which terms in a Boolean expression should be grouped (i.e., the order of the operations).

NOT. The Boolean operator (connector) that, when used with a term, eliminates the records containing that term. A minus sign immediately in front of a term can sometimes be substituted for the word "NOT."

OR. The Boolean operator (connector) that, when used between two terms, retrieves all records that contain either term.

portal (Web portal). Web services that position themselves as primary gateways for people to enter the Web, starting points for getting what one needs from the Web. In doing so, these services usually provide a variety of features to attract users to their sites, including search engines, directories, free e-mail, chat rooms, etc.

precision. In information retrieval, the degree to which a group of retrieved records actually match the searcher's needs. More technically, precision is the ratio of the number of relevant items retrieved to the total number of items retrieved (multiplied by 100 percent in order to express the ratio as a percentage). For example, if a query produced 10 records and 6 of them were judged relevant, the precision would be 60 percent. This is sometimes referred to as "relevance."

proximity. The nearness of two terms. Some search engines provide proximity operators, such as NEAR, which allow a user to specify how close two terms must be in order for a record containing those terms to be retrieved.

radio buttons. A feature on Web pages that allows you to make a choice by clicking a round "button." These are used when you have the option of only a single choice out of multiple choices (for example, to turn a feature either "on" or "off").

ranking. The process by which the display/output order of retrieved records is determined. Search engines use algorithms that evaluate records in order to assign a "score" to records, which is meant to be indicative of the relative "relevance" of each record. The retrieved records can then be ranked and listed on the basis of these scores.

recall. In information retrieval, the degree to which a search has actually managed to find all the relevant records in the database. More technically, it is the ratio of the number of relevant records that were retrieved to the total number of relevant records in the database (multiplied by 100 percent in order to express the ratio as a percentage). For example, if a query retrieved four relevant records, but there were 10 relevant records in the database, the recall for that search would be 40 percent. Recall is usually difficult to measure since the number of relevant records in a database is often very difficult to determine.

record. A unit of information in a database that contains items of related data. In an address book database, for example, each single record might be the collection of information about one individual person, such as name, address, ZIP code, phone, etc. In the databases of Web search engines, each record is the collection of information that describes a single Web page.

relevance. The degree to which a record matches the user's query (or the user's needs as expressed in a query). Search engines often assign relevance "scores" to each retrieved record, with the scores representing an estimate of the relevance of that record.

search engines. Programs that accept a user's query, search a database, and return to the user those records that match the query. The term is often used more broadly to refer not just to the information-retrieval program itself, but also to the interface and associated features, programs, and services.

spider. Programs that search the World Wide Web in order to identify new (or changed) pages for the purpose of adding those pages to a search service's database.

stop words. Small or frequently occurring words that an information-retrieval program doesn't bother to index (ostensibly because the words are "insignificant," but more likely because the indexing of those words would take up too much storage space or require too much processing).

streaming media. Media (audio, video) files that are designed so that the entire file does not have to be downloaded before the recipient can begin hearing or viewing it.

submitted URLs. URLs (Internet addresses) that a person directly submits to a search engine service in order to have that address and its associated Web page(s) added to the service's database.

syntax. The specific order of elements, notations, etc. by which instructions must be submitted to a computer search system.

thesaurus. A listing of terms usually showing the relationship between terms, such as whether one term is narrower or broader than another. Thesauri are used in information retrieval to identify related terms to be searched.

time-out. The amount of time a system will work on a task, or wait for results, before ceasing the task. Also referred to as "waiting time."

truncation. Feature in information-retrieval systems that allows one to search using the stem or root of a word and automatically retrieve records with all terms that begin with that string of characters. Truncation is usually specified using a symbol such as an asterisk. For example, in some Web search engines, town* would retrieve town, towns, township, etc.

URL. "Uniform Resource Locator"—The address by which a Web page can be located on the World Wide Web. URLs consist of several parts separated by periods and sometimes slashes.

Usenet. The world's largest system of Internet discussion groups (newsgroups).

vortal. Vertical market portal. A portal designed for users within a particular market, discipline, or other area of interest, with features such as news, links, etc. that are relevant to that particular market or topic.

waiting time. See "time-out."

THE AUTHOR
Randolph E. Hock, Ph.D.

Ran Hock specializes in creating and delivering customized courses that teach researchers to use the Internet effectively. Through his one-person company, Online Strategies (www.onstrat.com), his courses have been delivered to large and small companies, associations, libraries, schools, and government agencies. Hock has been a chemistry teacher, a chemistry librarian (at MIT), and the first data services librarian at the University of Pennsylvania. For many years he held training and management positions with DIALOG Information Services and Knight-Ridder Information. He lives in Vienna, Virginia, with his wife and two younger children and hopes to someday have time to again pursue his hobby of genealogy.

Index for The Extreme Searcher's Guide to Web Search Engines

More Great Books
from Information Today, Inc.

The Invisible Web

Uncovering Information Sources Search Engines Can't See

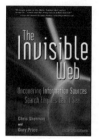

By Chris Sherman and Gary Price Foreword by Danny Sullivan

Most people are unaware that most of the authoritative information accessible over the Internet is invisible to search engines like AltaVista, HotBot, and Google. This invaluable material resides on the "Invisible Web," which is largely comprised of content-rich databases from universities, libraries, associations, businesses, and government agencies around the world. **CyberAge Books • Available:**
July 2001/softbound/ISBN 0-910965-51-X

$29.95

International Business Information on the Web

Searcher magazine's Guide to Sites and Strategies for Global Business Research

By Sheri R. Lanza
Edited and with a Foreword by Barbara Quint

Here is the first ready-reference for effective worldwide business research, written by experienced international business researcher Sheri R. Lanza and edited by *Searcher* magazine's Barbara Quint. This book helps readers identify overseas buyers, find foreign suppliers, investigate potential partners and competitors, uncover international market research and industry analysis, and much more.

CyberAge Books • Available: May 2001/380 pp/softbound ISBN 0-910965-46-3

$29.95

Super Searchers Go to the Source

The Interviewing and Hands-On Information Strategies of Top Primary Researchers—Online, on the Phone, and in Person

By Risa Sacks, Edited by Reva Basch

For the most focused, current, in-depth information on any subject, nothing beats going directly to the source—to the experts. This is "Primary Research," and it's the focus of the seventh title in the "Super Searchers" series. From the boardrooms of America's top corporations, to the halls of academia, to the pressroom of the *New York Times*, Risa Sacks interviews 12 of the best primary researchers in the business.

CyberAge Books • Available: September 2001/320 pp/softbound ISBN 0-910965-53-6

$24.95

Super Searchers on Mergers & Acquisitions

The Online Research Secrets of Top Corporate Researchers and M&A Pros

By Jan Davis Tudor • Edited by Reva Basch

The sixth title in the "Super Searchers" series is a unique resource for business owners, brokers, appraisers, entrepreneurs, and investors who use the Internet and online services to research Mergers & Acquisitions (M&A) opportunities. Leading business valuation researcher Jan Davis Tudor interviews 13 top M&A researchers, who share their secrets for finding, evaluating, and delivering critical deal-making data on companies and industries. As a reader bonus, "The Super Searchers Web Page" features links to the most important online information sources for M&A research.

CyberAge Books • 2001/208 pp/softbound/ISBN 0-910965-48-X • $24.95

The Quintessential Searcher

The Wit & Wisdom of Barbara Quint

Edited by Marylaine Block

Searcher Magazine editor Barbara Quint (bq) is not only one of the world's most famous online searchers, but the most creative and controversial writer, editor, and speaker to emerge from the information industry in the last two decades. Whether she's chastising database providers about unacceptable fees, interfaces, and updates; recounting the ills visited on the world by com-puter makers; or inspiring her readers to achieve greatness; her voice is consistently original and compelling. In this book, for the first time anywhere, hundreds of bq's most memorable, insightful, and politically incorrect quotations have been gathered for the enjoyment of her many fans.

Available: August 2001/220 pp/softbound/ISBN 1-57387-114-1 • $19.95

net.people

The Personalities and Passions Behind the Web Sites

By Eric C. Steinert and Thomas E. Bleier

With the explosive growth of the Internet, people everywhere are bringing their dreams and schemes to life as Web sites. In *net.people*, get up close and personal with the creators of 36 of the world's most intriguing online ventures. For the first time, these entrepreneurs and visionaries share their personal stories and hard-won secrets of Webmastering. You'll learn how all of them launched a home page, increased site traffic, geared up for e-commerce, found financing, dealt with failure and success, built new relationships—and discovered that a Web site had changed their lives forever.

CyberAge Books • 2000/317 pp/softbound/ISBN 0-910965-37-4 • $19.95

The Modem Reference, 4th Edition
The Complete Guide to PC Communications

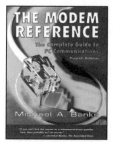

By Michael A. Banks

Now in its 4th edition, this popular handbook explains the concepts behind computer data, data encoding, and transmission, providing practical advice for PC users who want to get the most from their online operations. In his uniquely readable style, author and techno-guru Michael A. Banks (*The Internet Unplugged*) takes readers on a tour of PC data communications technology, explaining how modems, fax machines, computer networks, and the Internet work. He provides an in-depth look at how data is communicated between computers all around the world, demystifying the terminology, hardware, and software. *The Modem Reference* is a must-read for students, professional online users, and all computer users who want to maximize their PC fax and data communications capabilities.

CyberAge Books • 2000/306 pp/softbound/ISBN 0-910965-36-6 • $29.95

Internet Business Intelligence
How to Build a Big Company System on a Small Company Budget

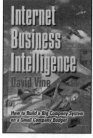

By David Vine

According to author David Vine, business success in the competitive, global marketplace of the 21st century will depend on a firm's ability to use information effectively—and the most successful firms will be those that harness the Internet to create and maintain a powerful information edge. In *Internet Business Intelligence*, Vine explains how any company—large or small—can build a complete, low-cost, Internet-based business intelligence system that really works. If you're fed up with Internet hype and wondering, "Where's the beef?," you'll appreciate this savvy, no-nonsense approach to using the Internet to solve everyday business problems and stay one step ahead of the competition.

CyberAge Books • 2000/448 pp/softbound/ISBN 0-910965-35-8 • $29.95

Millennium Intelligence
Understanding and Conducting Competitive Intelligence in the Digital Age

Edited by Jerry P. Miller

With contributions from the world's leading business intelligence practitioners, here is a tremendously informative and practical look at the CI process, how it is changing, and how it can be managed effectively in the Digital Age. Loaded with case studies, tips, and techniques.

CyberAge Books • 2000/276 pp/softbound/ISBN 0-910965-28-5 $29.95

Internet Blue Pages

The Guide to Federal Government
Web Sites, 2001–2002 Edition

Edited by Laurie Andriot

Internet Blue Pages (*IBP*) is the leading guide to federal government information on the Web. *IBP 2001-2002* includes over 1,800 annotated agency listings, arranged in U.S. Government Manual style to help you find the information you need. Entries include agency name and URL, function or purpose of selected agencies, and links from agency home pages. With double the coverage of the previous edition, *IBP* now includes federal courts, military libraries, Department of Energy libraries, Federal Reserve banks, presidential libraries, national parks, and Social Security offices. A companion Web site features regularly updated agency links.

CyberAge Books • 2000/464 pp/softbound/ISBN 0-910965-43-9
$34.95

Electronic Democracy, 2nd Edition

Using the Internet to Transform
American Politics

By Graeme Browning
Foreword by Adam Clayton Powell III

In this new edition of *Electronic Democracy,* award-winning journalist and author Graeme Browning details the colorful history of politics and the Net, describes the key Web-based sources of political information, offers practical techniques for influencing legislation online, and provides a fascinating, realistic vision of the future.

CyberAge Books • Available: September 2001/260 pp
softbound ISBN 0-910965-41-2
$19.95